George B. McClellan
The Disposable
Patriot

Michael J. McHugh

Arlington Heights, Illinois
Christian Liberty Press
1998

Printed by
Christian Liberty Press

502 West Euclid Avenue
Arlington Heights, Illinois 60004
www.homeschools.org

Cover design and graphics by Eric D. Bristley
Layout and copyediting by Edward J. Shewan
Set in Garamond
Printed in the United States of America

ISBN 1-930092-15-6

Acknowledgment

Special thanks are extended to the West Point Museum Collections, U.S. Military Academy, for granting us permission to utilize
the image of George B. McClellan located on the front cover of
this book.

Preface

It is my firm belief that individuals who love liberty need to be exposed to the lives of great and good American patriots. The life of General George Brinton McClellan is worthy of just such attention, for it helps to remind us that truly great Americans are those who seek to do what is in the best interest of God and country.

In this biographical sketch of the famous Civil War general, George B. McClellan, I have attempted to portray his military genius, uprightness of conduct, and firm belief in an overruling Providence. These traits of character formed the cornerstone upon which McClellan's legacy was founded, and upon which young people of our day would do well to build.

This book is respectfully presented to the public in the hope that it will bless the lives of all who read it.

Michael J. McHugh
Arlington Heights, Illinois

Contents

"A Union that can only be maintained by swords and bayonets, and in which strife and civil war are to take the place of brotherly love and kindness, has no charm for me."

—ROBERT E. LEE

Introduction

A certain degree of patience and persistence is required when studying the life of General George Brinton McClellan. After all, this military legend is unquestionably one of the most complex and controversial figures in all of American history. The difficulty in understanding the life of General McClellan is due, in part, to the fact that his career was at its height during the turbulent period of the War Between the States—a time when passions were commonly apt to distract the true nature of people and events.

McClellan, both during and after his life, has been subjected to a great deal of partisan analysis. This conservative and patriotic soldier has been both idolized as a military genius and condemned as a cowardly "do-nothing" failure. Those parties who identify with his view of the war tend to give him almost universal praise, while individuals who dislike his wartime politics and tactics commonly attempt to vilify his every thought and action. One of the goals of the following text is to set forth a balanced and true history of a great American without resorting to extremes.

In addition to the military exploits of George McClellan, this biography will delve into a careful analysis of his character and religious convictions. It is the view of the author that a clear understanding of any personality of history is not possible without first considering his spiritual principles and priorities. Virtually all references to George McClellan in print today either ignore or denigrate the profound influence that Christianity had upon his career.

At the age of thirty-four, George McClellan was suddenly named commander of the largest army in the Union and would soon thereafter be named supreme commander of all the Northern armies. These events, and the battles that followed, would thrust

General McClellan into a constant sea of conflict both on and off the battlefield.

A great deal of the public and private correspondence issued by General McClellan survived the War, and, consequently, provides students of history with a solid basis on which to evaluate his wartime experiences and attitudes. The vast majority of the material which comprises this biography is taken directly from the writings of McClellan himself as well as from other official government reports or records. Helpful commentary is also included from individuals who fought alongside General McClellan.

It was George Washington who wrote the following rule for living when he was a young man, "When a person does all that he can do to succeed in a noble endeavor, and yet fails, do not blame him for trying." As we will soon note, this wise proverb has not been applied to the man known as George Brinton McClellan. Historians have commonly enjoyed trashing the memory of this godly, principled military leader because he took on a noble and difficult endeavor while failing to live up to their expectations.

May Almighty God use this biography to honor the memory of a decent and talented soldier, who risked his career, his family's security, his reputation, and even his life to do what he felt the Lord had called him to do—preserve the Union and with it the God-given liberties of its citizens.

Chapter One

Birth and Early Days

1826–1842

George Brinton McClellan was born in Philadelphia, Pennsylvania on December 3, 1826. His ancestors came from Scotland to the American Colonies in the early 1700s. The great-grandfather of little George was named Samuel McClellan. He immigrated from Scotland to the colony of Connecticut and soon became a distinguished soldier and adventurer. He fought with the American militia during the War for American Independence. Some accounts place him at the battle of Bunker Hill. This brave patriot rose to the rank of brigadier general by 1779. General Samuel McClellan had two sons, James and John, who founded a private school in Woodstock, Connecticut. These men lived and worked their whole lives in this part of the newly formed Union of States.

James McClellan married and raised a family in Connecticut. His wife gave birth to two boys named George and Samuel. George McClellan and his brother were gifted students. They began to study science and medicine as they grew up in Connecticut. George graduated from Yale College in 1816 and went on to earn his degree in medicine from the University of Philadelphia. This gentleman was a leader in the field of medicine and a respected surgeon. Many of his leisure hours were spent training and grooming a fine stable of race horses.

Dr. George McClellan moved to the city of Philadelphia shortly after his graduation from medical school in 1819. It was at this time that Dr. McClellan decided to marry Elizabeth Brinton who came from a wealthy and influential family in Philadelphia. They were married in 1820 at the local Presbyterian church where they were members. Dr. McClellan and his bride were devout Christians who often associated with godly individuals in Philadelphia such as Daniel Webster.

**George B. McClellan as a New Lieutenant
with His Father and Sister, Mary**

George and Elizabeth McClellan were blessed with two daughters and three sons during their long and happy years of marriage. The second son born to this couple was named George Brinton McClellan, Jr. As we have already noted, George was born on a cold and snowy December day in the year 1826. Elizabeth McClellan made every effort to see that little George, and the other children, received the best possible education. At the age of five, George was sent to an infant school and then spent four years in a private school run by Sears Cook Walker. Mr. Walker was a gifted scientist and Harvard graduate. After George reached the age of ten, he was tutored at home by a one-eyed teacher by the name of Schiffer. Mr. Schiffer was a magnificent German classical scholar who required his pupils to converse in French and Latin. As a consequence, young George McClellan became well-versed in classical literature, history studies, and grammar.

George received additional schooling at a private academy run by Reverend Samuel W. Crawford during 1838 and 1839. This excellent early education enabled George Brinton McClellan to enroll into the University of Pennsylvania at the age of thirteen.

At the encouragement of his father, George began to pursue a course of study in law at the University level. After two years of study, however, George changed his focus from law to a military career.

In the spring of 1842, George's father wrote to the Secretary of War and to President John Tyler in an effort to help his son gain an appointment to the American Military Academy at West Point. After some brief delays, George was able to gain the needed congressional nomination and acceptance even though he was only fifteen years old.[1] Cadet McClellan arrived at West Point in June 1842, and, on the first of July, he was officially received into the class of 1846.

President John Tyler

---

1. The normal age requirement was sixteen.

Chapter Two

Little Mac Enters West Point

1842–1846

Shortly after arriving at the Military Academy, George began to feel depressed and homesick. He wrote his parents in Philadelphia that he felt as alone and abandoned "as if in a boat in the middle of the Atlantic." Perhaps his young age accounted for some of his homesickness, but it is even more likely that his sadness was due to his lack of satisfaction with his performance during his initial marching and riding drills. He occasionally wrote about how disgusted he was to be the smallest cadet in his class and how he resented having to endure the harsh orders of smug upperclassmen who cared little if he succeeded.

Slowly, however, he began to gain confidence as his marching and physical prowess began to improve. By the opening of his academic or classroom studies in September 1842, George McClellan was beginning to feel at home at the Academy.

For most cadets, the first year of study at West Point was nothing less than agony. Each day presented nine or ten hours of intense study in advanced mathematics and French, along with two or three hours of drills and field exercises. George McClellan, however, was not your average cadet; his early education and gifted mind made the rigorous academic challenges at the Academy seem quite manageable. Before the end of Cadet McClellan's first year, many cadets and instructors were speculating that George would wind up at the top of his class.

Only eighty-three of the original 134 cadets, who comprised the class of 1846, survived the first year at West Point. Several notable classmates, such as Thomas J. Jackson and Ambrose P. Hill were barely able to pass the first year program due to their lack of early education and poor study skills.

Little Mac, as he was sometimes called, not only survived his first year at the Academy, he began to excel as a boy wonder. His excellent family background and training made him into a gentleman, and he soon began to mix with the more cultured cadets at West Point. It is interesting to note that Cadet McClellan seemed to prefer the companionship of cadets from the Southern States. "Almost all my associates—indeed all of them—are Southerners; I am sorry to say that the manners, feelings, and opinions of the Southerners are far, far preferable to those of the majority of the Northerners at this place," wrote McClellan to his brother John. Indeed, with the exception of the issue of a state's right to secede from the Union, there never was much to separate George McClellan's views from the average Southerner.

Cadet McClellan had only one primary gripe at this point in his West Point experience, and he was certainly not alone in his complaint—the food! Stale bread, hard peas, and tough meat were difficult for most cadets to endure. Many of the cadets came from prosperous farms or wealthy families and were not accustomed to "army chow." It was not uncommon for students to write home

West Point in the 1840s

requesting apples, cheese, or anything fresh that could supplement the "trash" that they were confronted with each day in the mess hall.

During the second year of study, cadets completed more geometry and calculus classes in preparation for the advanced engineering and science courses that would confront them in their last two years at the Academy. French language studies continued for the primary purpose of equipping cadets to be able to read French military and engineering reports. Cadets also received two years of drawing instruction to prepare them for future work in the field of military and civilian engineering. Drawing was one of the few classes in which McClellan did not move to the top of his class.

Not surprisingly, the major theme of Academy life was order and discipline. Reveille could be heard at five in the morning. A drum was used to signal the key activities of each day. Even the call for church or chapel services, where attendance was required by faculty and cadets alike, was by drum. A long and detailed code of regulations "more rigorous than those of the book of Deuteronomy" faced the cadet daily. Each and every breach of Academy rules typically brought the erring cadet a demerit or two. More than a few cadets were sent home as a result of excessive demerits.

Cadets at West Point in the 1840's

The even-tempered and disciplined character of George McClellan kept him out of demerit trouble. Erasmus Keyes, an artillery instructor at the Academy, was so impressed with Little Mac that he wrote, "a pleasanter pupil was never called to the blackboard." Dabney Maury, one of

McClellan's friends from Virginia, commented that his classmate had "every evidence of gentle nature and high culture, and his countenance was as charming as his demeanor was modest and winning."

During his third year of study, McClellan was still chasing Charles Stewart for the top position in the class of 1846. Cadet McClellan complained to his mother that "I do not get marked as well for as good (or better) recitation, as the man above me … if I were already above him, I could distance him, I think." Little Mac determined to wind up at the top of his class before his fourth year began.

Many of the letters and comments that were written by George McClellan during this point in his life reveal a chronic tendency to dwell on the fact that life is not always fair or equitable. This character flaw, perhaps stemming from the prideful notion that he was destined for greatness, followed him much of his adult life. It sometimes made him interpret the comments or actions of others in a childish manner, as if every circumstance in life was merely calculated to help or hurt the interests of George McClellan, Jr.

His lack of maturity was also compounded by a superficial commitment to the Christian faith that was largely perfunctory. The church services he attended and his general outward moral tendencies were, in large measure, the result of good habits that were engraved in him while under his parents direct care. McClellan himself, admits that he occasionally came drunk to some of the special church services that were presented during the Christmas season at West Point. It was not until the age of 32 that George McClellan was brought to a fuller and deeper commitment to the Christian faith.

The fourth and final year quickly unfolded for the class of 1846. This year was commonly regarded by senior cadets as the most interesting part of their course of study at West Point. Considerable time was spent studying infantry and artillery tactics, ethics, constitutional and international law, logic, military engineering, and the science of war. George McClellan was extremely fond of studying the science of war and made good use of his French language skills to pore over popular French military journals.

During the spring of McClellan's final year, he began to think about what branch of military service would be appropriate for him. He was quite certain that he would graduate at or near the top of his class and would, therefore, have his choice of assignments. At this same time, rumors of war were beginning to move through West Point as government leaders in the United States began to argue with Mexico about the territory of Texas.

Although Cadet McClellan vowed to finish first in his class, he would have to settle for second place behind the gifted Charles

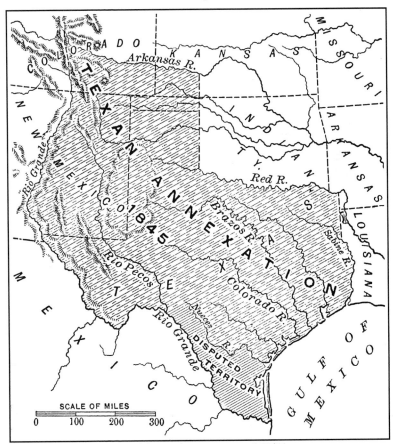

The Texan Annexation of 1845

Stewart. As the year drew to a close, fifty-nine cadets had survived the four-year ordeal at West Point. This was the largest graduating class in West Point's forty-four-year history. The backwards man from Virginia, Thomas Jackson, surprised everyone by finishing seventeenth in his class. Many of his classmates remarked that, "if we stay here another year, Old Jack will be head of the class."

The stern and earnest Jackson would have surprised many of his friends at West Point, if they had known what he told his sister at the time of graduation. He wrote her stating, "It grieves me to think that in a short time, I must be separated from amiable and meritorious friends whom an acquaintance of years has endeared to me by many ties." Jackson but expressed the feelings that were on the heart of many of the class of 1846. Like most graduating classes from West Point, they were apprehensive because of the new duties and cares that loomed before their youthful faces. They were, however, excited on account of the opportunities that lay before them.

The graduates of 1846 would now take their military careers, with all of its cares, into the ranks of the United States Army. Each graduate would receive the rank of brevet (brə•vēt′) second lieutenant until he could be formally commissioned into the regular army officer corps as openings became available.

As valedictorian of the Dialectic Society, McClellan was privileged to present the keynote speech before this prestigious group on the eve of graduation in June 1846. During his address, he reminded the audience that literary pursuits were "essential to the man who would bear the character of an accomplished and polished gentleman ..." The main theme of his speech, however, was preoccupied with admonitions regarding the dangers of the growing sectionalism that was beginning to gain momentum in the United States. He warned his listeners that:

> If party or sectional spirit should rise so high as to bring upon us the horrors of civil war,... let the army, united as one man, throw its weight into the scale, and the result cannot be doubtful.... Let us hope that the army will ever incline to the conservative party, to that one whose motto shall be 'The Union, one and indivisible'.

McClellan concluded his talk, as would Abraham Lincoln during the War Between the States, with a phrase from the Gospel of Mark— "A house divided against itself, must surely fall."

Abraham Lincoln

The thoughts of all Americans quickly turned to war in May 1846 as President James Polk requested that Congress declare the United States at war with Mexico. McClellan, after hearing the news, wrote to his sister Frederica,

Hip! hip! Hurrah! War at last sure enough! Ain't it glorious!... Well, it appears that our wishes have at last been gratified and we shall soon have the intense satisfaction of fighting the crowd—mosquitoes and Mexicans.... You have no idea in what a state of excitement we have been here.

Like most youthful graduates from West Point, George McClellan would view the Mexican War as a gift from God, particularly designed to advance the military careers of needy junior officers. One thing was for sure, it was much easier to get promoted during wartime conditions than in times of peace.

It would only take a few weeks for George McClellan to secure a commission as second lieutenant in an engineering company—just the type of assessment desired by Little Mac as he readied himself for a nice little war in Mexico.

Lieutenant George B. McClellan

Chapter Three

A Nice Little War in Mexico

1846–1848

In early July of 1846, the newly commissioned officer of Engineers, George McClellan, received orders to return to West Point to help train and organize a company of one hundred soldiers bound for Mexico. The United States government decided to establish a new training and staging center at West Point so that more men could be prepared for war.

It would take McClellan and his fellow officers two months to whip these new troops into shape. The men were trained in infantry and rifle tactics as well as in the classic skills of the military engineer. In these days, an engineer company was expected to support the advance of the army by building pontoon bridges, erecting forts or bunkers, or simply constructing better roads. Lieutenant McClellan was very pleased with the progress of his men. He boasted that his troops could build a pontoon bridge as quickly as the famous French corps of pontoniers. McClellan was quick to predict that his company would "astonish the natives if they will only give us half a chance."

Much to the delight of Lieutenant McClellan, his company finally set sail from New York City on September 26, 1846, bound for the "seat of war" in Mexico. The journey to Brazos de Santiago, Texas, took fourteen days and ended up at a crude port that boasted nothing more than sand and a large mosquito population.

On September 24, the Mexican soldiers who had been fighting at Monterey surrendered. They had been defeated by the small American army that was already at work in northern Mexico. General Taylor, who commanded the first contingent of soldiers in Mexico, was able to secure the disputed border between Texas and Mexico but there still remained a large Mexican army that was ready to fight. An armistice had been agreed to at this time in the hopes of ending the conflict without further bloodshed. The Mexican government, however, would simply use this brief period of weeks to rebuild their broken armies.

During this temporary lull in the fighting, thousands of United States troops continued to arrive in Mexico from various staging areas. McClellan moved the engineers of Company A to a military assembly area near Camargo, Mexico. Lieutenant McClellan rode at the head of his troops along with Captain Swift and "Legs" Smith. Mac carried two revolvers, a saber, a double-barred shotgun, and a bowie knife. Like most West Point officers, he came prepared to meet trouble head on.

General Zachary Taylor

By the end of 1846, nearly thirty of McClellan's West Point classmates had arrived in Mexico. It was strange for McClellan to be so quickly reunited with old comrades such as Jimmy Stuart (his old roommate), Dabney Maury, and of course, Thomas Jackson. As it turned out, it was a tremendous benefit for McClellan to have his friends close, for trouble was at hand. The trouble came not from the Mexicans but from the mosquitoes.

While General Taylor was waiting for orders to come from Washington, Lieutenant McClellan contracted malaria and dysentery. He was confined to a hospital bed for almost one month while being nursed back to health by his friend, Jimmy Stuart. The one consolation for George McClellan was that his unit was largely idle during his period of illness. The malaria that McClellan experienced in Mexico, however, would stay with him for the rest of his life. He would often refer to this problem as his "Mexican disease" when it flared up from time-to-time.

General Winfield Scott

After McClellan recovered in the middle of November, the focus of the conflict in Mexico underwent a dramatic change. Suddenly the United States forces were reoriented from a defensive army to an army of invasion. The leaders in Washington were convinced that the temporary armistice has been only serving the interest of the Mexican army. They demanded a new offensive posture to the war effort, and directed the army's general-in-chief Winfield Scott to coordinate a decisive invasion of Mexico.

The army of General Scott was staged and organized at Tampico during the winter of 1846–47 as final arrangements were being completed for the invasion. Scott went to great lengths to secure the services of experienced West Point officers. Perhaps the best known officer was the noble and dutiful Robert E. Lee who graduated from West Point in 1829. Another famous southern military leader who would fight along with the likes of Lee and McClellan was Lieutenant Pierre Gustave Toutant Beauregard.

General Scott decided to throw his entire army in one massive assault against Mexico City itself. He planned to land his army at the port of Veracruz and march up the main road leading to the capital—260 miles in all. This plan was neither original nor shrewd—but it met with the approval of the leaders at Washington.

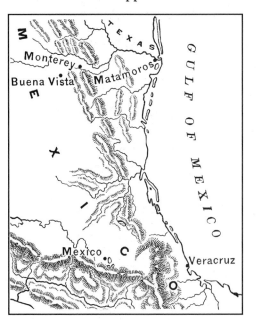

Map of Eastern Mexico

The initial advance of the invasion force to Tampico, Mexico went smoothly, and McClellan's only headaches were limited to his constant struggle to keep his volunteer soldiers in line. George McClellan frequently referred to these men as the "confounded voluntario." "They don't know the butt from the muzzle of a musket," bellowed McClellan.

During these days of further training and waiting, McClellan would often have time to write home to the folks in Philadelphia. He wrote his mother stating, "You never saw such a merry group as we are—no care, no trouble—we criticize the generals—laugh and swear at the mustangs and volunteers...." He closed his statements to his mother by explaining the liberty that was granted to the regular officers in terms of their freedom to sleep or rise as they pleased. He also was amused by the fact that, "When we have cigars, we smoke them; when we have none, we go without; when we have brandy, we drink it; when we have not, we make it up by laughing at our predicament—that is the way we live." It is quite evident by the letters of young George McClellan that he quite enjoyed the unchristian atmosphere that was part of his life as a combat officer. Not all of the invasion troops appreciated the social life in camp as much as George McClellan, for many of the men were bored and wanted a little warfare.

The time soon arrived for the 13,000 man expeditionary force to sail to the port city of Veracruz. Much to the delight of McClellan and his fellow invaders, there was a distinct lack of Mexican resistance during their landing at Veracruz in early March 1847. From the time that McClellan and his engineers reached shore, until the formal siege at Veracruz was successfully completed, Little Mac was busy building barricades and bunkers. It took until March 27 before the Mexicans in Veracruz were ready to surrender. For over one week, the Americans had rained thousands of cannonballs and howitzer shells—250 tons worth in all—upon the fortress city of Veracruz. The occupants of this besieged city gave up the fight.

Little time was wasted after the surrender at Veracruz, for General Scott was anxious to get his army moving down the road to Mexico City. By April 13, the entire expeditionary force was under foot and headed for their main objective. The engineer soldiers primary task during the weary march toward Mexico City was to outfit roads and battery positions for the advancing infantry and artillery. McClellan rode in advance of the main body of troops to scout out the roads that lay ahead.

It was during this scouting excursion that the young lieutenant came under fire for the first time. McClellan wrote that the bullets came "whistling like hail" around his head as Mexican troopers took their aim. "Thank God that they can't shoot straight," wrote McClellan to his friends back home.

General Scott's army proceeded almost fifty miles toward their objective before being attacked by a large 12,000 man Mexican army commanded by General Santa Anna. The Mexican leaders decided to attack the Americans from a steep 1,000-foot hill next to the city of Cerro Gordo. The road leading up to this town passed through a narrow gorge appropriately called the Devil's Jaws. Santa

Anna hoped to trap and destroy large numbers of Americans at this spot. It certainly appeared to many observers that the American army was caught in a trap that might force them to abandon their mission.

General Santa Anna of Mexico

General Scott received a bold plan of action from Captain Robert E. Lee and Lieutenant Beauregard, who performed some daring forward reconnaissances to determine the position of the enemy. Scott approved the battle plan of Lee by ordering a large detachment of men and artillery to move through a narrow mountain pass on the left flank of the Mexican army. To distract the Mexicans, Scott ordered the rest of his army to stage a phony attack on the right flank of Santa Anna. Much to the disgust of Lieutenant McClellan, he was ordered to support the phony attack on the right. McClellan naturally wished to stay with Captain Lee and his engineer troopers, but an officer must, above all, obey his orders.

The attack by Lee on the left flank was extremely successful. The Americans were able to position three large cannons on the top of a hill overlooking Cerro Gordo and they pounded the Mexican army mercilessly. By the 19th of April, Santa Anna and his shattered army had fled their positions. The battle of Cerro Gordo was a key victory for the American expeditionary force. Lieutenant McClellan distinguished himself during the battle and was mentioned by name in a report sent to Washington by General Scott.

After the surrender at Cerro Gordo, Scott's army was able to continue down the main road towards Mexico City. They soon approached the town of Jalapa, a beautiful and lush city forty-five hundred feet above the Gulf of Mexico. The campaign of General Scott suddenly came to an abrupt halt, however, after his troops reached Jalapa. Over one-third of his volunteer soldiers decided to return to the United States on account of the fact that their enlistment term had expired. Scott was obviously outraged, but he had no ability to force these volunteers to stay.

What remained of Scott's army, about 7,000 men, were moved to the town of Puebla so as to move closer to their objective. At this place, Scott would wait for reinforcements before pressing on with his campaign. The only exploit of McClellan at Puebla involved his capture of a Mexican cavalry captain single-handedly. McClellan and his fellow soldiers were still seventy miles away from Mexico City as they garrisoned at Puebla.

While stationed at this large city, McClellan visited a local Catholic seminary in an effort to locate a book about the conquest of Mexico by Cortez. He had been told that the Americans were following essentially the same route as Cortez. McClellan eventually purchased a book on Cortez while he was at the seminary "searching for something readable among their shelves of bad theology."

George McClellan's stay at Puebla was marked by personal tragedy, as a letter arrived from Philadelphia announcing the death of his father. His dad had died quite unexpectedly, at the age of fifty. This sad news was naturally a major blow to McClellan. For several days he was unwilling to speak and would not be comforted. Months later, he would write his brother John stating that his father was "as noble a being as ever graced the earth." He also agreed to assume partial responsibility for the sizable debts that his father left with the family.

By August 7, reinforcements had reached Scott in Puebla bringing his troop strength up to 10,000 men. He wanted to have a considerably larger force before assaulting Mexico City, but he would have to settle for being outnumbered three to one.

Route of the United States Army During the Mexican War

The next day, thousands of American soldiers, including a brigade of cavalry and a siege train, were headed for the capital of Mexico. McClellan and his engineers were ordered to scout the area surrounding the village of Contreras where Santa Anna was rumored to have placed his army. Due to the extremely foolish orders of General Gideon Pillow, who was commanding McClellan's engineers, hundreds of men were sent unsupported into enemy fire. By some miracle of grace, Lieutenant McClellan escaped death even though two horses were shot out from under him during the day's battle. On one occasion during the battle, shrapnel from a shell literally bounced off McClellan's sword and bruised him. The following day, McClellan had yet another opportunity to distinguish himself under fire. General Scott ordered a headlong assault on the town of Cherubusco, and McClellan's unit was in the thick of the fight. McClellan would earn a field promotion to first lieutenant "for gallant and meritorious conduct" on the battlefield at Cherubusco. In the official report of the battle, Brigadier Persifor F. Smith noted that, "Nothing seemed to G. W. Smith or McClellan too bold to be undertaken or too difficult to be executed."

Only one major obstacle lay between Scott's army and Mexico City—the fortress known as Chapultepec. McClellan and his engineers began to establish a series of four batteries for the siege guns that would batter the Mexican fortress. Beginning on September 11, McClellan set to work under the direction of Robert E. Lee to complete this important project. The engineers completed their work by September 13, and had the gun emplacements ready to support the infantry assault on Chapultepec.

The huge siege cannons began pounding the castlelike fortress at Chapultepec. The main assault began the next morning as four hundred men with long ladders charged the western wall of the Mexican fortress. Another storming party, under the command of Colonel Joseph E. Johnston, attacked the front gate of Chapultepec under heavy fire. Thomas Jackson led an artillery assault on the left side of the Mexicans, exposing himself to extreme danger on a regular basis. Cannonballs and shots were flying all around him, while Jackson almost single-handedly destroyed a battery of Mexican cannons that were protecting the heights above the fort.

Wave after wave of American infantry advanced to the walls around Chapultepec. Lieutenant James Longstreet and George E. Pickett, who in later years would become famous as Confederate generals, were among the first soldiers to scale the wall and raise the American flag upon the top of the Mexican fort. Men fell in great numbers as they fought each other in hand-to-hand combat. After an hour of fierce fighting, the Mexican general Santa Anna ordered a general retreat of his army toward Mexico City. Although the American troops were battle weary, General Scott knew that he must press his men forward to capture the Mexican capital.

As the Mexican army streamed toward their capital, McClellan volunteered to join an infantry division under Commander William Worth. This unit pursued the enemy to the very gates of Mexico City. McClellan led an attack upon the Mexicans as his unit pressed on toward their objective. For the first time, Lieutenant McClellan experienced hand-to-hand combat in a desperate attempt to reach the walls around Mexico City. Mexican soldiers would often position themselves in tiny houses outside the city limits, and shoot at the advancing Americans. An hour before sunset, McClellan and his comrades were able to break through the walls of several homes with picks and shovels and overtake the soldiers inside these positions. Artillery support was provided by infantry quartermaster Ulysses S. Grant as the rooftops of the Mexican homes were cleared of snipers by his cannon fire.

The American forces had penetrated the Mexican capital at several points and had secured the gates to the city as the morning of September 14 unfolded. General Scott had planned the final attack upon the center of Mexico City, and his brave band was poised to make the last assault. Much to the surprise and joy of every American soldier, however, a delegation from the city came out under a flag of surrender. Several hours later, the American flag was flying proudly over the citadel of Mexico City. Santa Anna had fled with most of his army during the night hours and would not return. Several days later, the Mexicans would attempt to besiege the American garrison at Puebla, but this action was defeated in short order. The fighting was officially over!

McClellan wrote his brother John a few days after the battle stating, "Thank God! Our name has not suffered, so far, at my hands." Quite clearly, George McClellan had made the most of his opportunities. He, like so many others from the halls of West Point, had distinguished himself at every point of the campaign. His actions would earn him a second field promotion to the rank of Captain. At this point in Little Mac's life, however, he could only feel relief that he had survived with his honor intact. One of McClellan's comrades overheard him say, "Here we are—the deed is done—I am only glad no one can say 'poor Mac' over me."

In May 1848, a treaty of peace was signed between Mexico and the United States. Mexico agreed to hand over the territory of California, Texas, and New Mexico. George McClellan finally returned to West Point with his unit on June 22 amidst a hero's welcome. Much to his embarrassment, the citizens of Philadelphia honored him with a presentation sword and a hearty round of applause. All in all, it had been a nice little war!

Chapter Four

A Peacetime Soldier

1848–1857

Few of the soldiers who fought in the Mexican War were prepared to adjust to the tranquillity of a peacetime existence. They all had tasted life on the edge, and those who survived the intense experience of combat in foreign lands wanted the ride to last a lot longer.

For George McClellan, he would spend the next three years of his life (June '48–June '51) as a teaching assistant at West Point. Most of his time was spent training the company of engineers that was stationed at the Military Academy facility. He taught two classes to his trainees—practical engineering and mathematics.

This period of McClellan's life was characterized by a combination of restlessness and spiritual apathy. Almost from the beginning of his time at West Point, McClellan would occupy his time in petty arguments with Academy administrators as well as in vain amusements. As many young men before him, George McClellan would have to suffer the consequences of indulging a view of life that was based upon little more than pride and selfish ambition. In short, Mac was a frustrated young man who lacked the spiritual maturity to wait upon the Lord he claimed to love.

McClellan made numerous attempts to transfer his military post away from West Point. "Nothing whatever of the slightest importance, in this branch, can ever be done at this post," argued George McClellan to his military supervisors. He also found time to criticize the superintendent at the Academy for attempting to enforce the policy that required all personnel to attend chapel services. McClellan was apparently too busy worrying and fussing about his future to attend worship services. He did, however, make time for fun and games with friends.

Not surprisingly, most of McClellan's leisure time was spent with old military buddies such as Dabney Maury. This young Virginian would bring his hunting dogs with him as he visited his friend Mac at West Point. Both men loved to hunt, fish, and ride their horses all over the surrounding countryside. McClellan would write his sister-in-law about the benefits he received from these pursuits, "what pleasure it is to get with some comrade of the war and talk ('gas' as we say) over old times." Maury would later write McClellan about those visits recalling how "the slightest excuse was enough to begin popping corks... remember how you and I went to church tight [inebriated] on Christmas Eve...."

By the grace of God, these years of youthful vanity and indiscretion would soon be a thing of the past. The Lord had greater and higher purposes for this gifted and yet frustrated soldier.

During the last year in which Mac was stationed at West Point, he took advantage of a postgraduate course in the art of war taught by Dennis Hart Mahan. This professor also sponsored a "Napoleon Club" in which McClellan was active. In the spring of 1851, Mac completed a 111-page report about two of Napoleon's most famous battles. This activity was of genuine benefit to McClellan who desperately needed some quality intellectual stimulation. He would tell his sister Maria that the club members "compliment me by saying that my report gave a clear explanation of the campaign, so I am contented."

Mac also took the time to keep up with current events and the political scene. He followed with interest the debates that lead to the Compromise of 1850, which would bring California in as a free state while permitting the citizens of the newly acquired Mexican territories to decide whether they would or would not permit slavery. This act also strengthened the laws regarding the treatment of fugitive slaves, requiring that runaway slaves be returned to the slave states from which they fled.

George McClellan was staunchly conservative and pro-union in every respect. Although he was opposed to slavery in principle, he believed that the institution of slavery should be dealt with through political dialogue and orderly constitutional processes. In other words, he believed that the Union and civil tranquillity should not be jeopardized in the interest of trying to achieve a speedy end to slavery. He sincerely believed that the radical abolitionists were as dangerous to the cause of the Union as the extreme nationalists or secessionists in the South.

During June 1851, McClellan finally received the transfer he desired. He was ordered to leave his post at West Point for Fort Delaware. This fort was situated on a large island on the Delaware River, about forty miles south of Philadelphia. The work there, although somewhat obscure, was pleasant enough for George and he quickly fell into a new routine. Shortly after arriving at Fort Delaware, Mac learned that his best friend, Jimmy Stuart, had died in the Oregon wilderness fighting Indians. Stuart was just twenty-six years old and was one of several West Point graduates to die in the Indian Wars.

During the opening months of 1852, McClellan was stationed at the city of Washington to translate a French bayonet manual for publication by the War department. Shortly before the project was completed, Mac wrote to his commander General Totten requesting a new assignment. In the providence of God, a new and challenging assignment was soon placed before him.

McClellan was ordered to report for duty by April 1 at Fort Smith, Arkansas. He would serve as engineer, and second-in-command on an expedition to explore the Red River region bordering Oklahoma and Texas. The expedition would involve seventy-five men under the command of Captain Randolph B. Marcy and would largely be a fact finding mission to inform government officials of the suitability of this wilderness territory for settlement.

Shortly after leaving the last frontier fort, McClellan wrote his mother to report that he had finally met a superior officer who was worthy of his respect. He wrote, "Randolph Marcy is one of the finest men I ever met with, and never saw one better fitted to conduct such an expedition." McClellan was about as happy as he had been in years. He wrote his brother John on May 7 stating that he would not have missed this expedition for anything in the world. "The scenery equals in beauty and wildness any that I ever beheld."

Other than a few close encounters with Indians and rattlesnakes, Mac had a fairly calm tour of duty as a frontier pathfinder. The greatest excitement that his party encountered was when they reached a small frontier outpost on July 28. They were informed by officials at this outpost that a story had been circulated across the country stating that their expedition had been massacred by thousands of Comanches. This erroneous story had evidently been front page news in many parts of the country!

After returning to Arkansas with Captain Marcy, McClellan finalized his reports and handed over the mineral samples that he had collected during the expedition. He then received new orders to report to General Smith who was stationed on the Gulf Coast in Texas. A few days later, Mac bid farewell to his beloved friend and comrade Randolph Marcy and headed for Texas.

For almost two months, McClellan rode around the southern regions of Texas with General Smith inspecting frontier military posts. He truly enjoyed the role of explorer and frontiersman. It was just the lifestyle he needed to defeat his great enemy—idleness. He wrote his mother from San Antonio, "the very short rest of one week I've had here only makes me long for the march again.... I can't stand inactivity." During one of his rare periods of inaction, McClellan received a copy of the first book he translated, entitled *Bayonet Exercise*. He was grateful to see his work in print.

In late October 1852, Mac received orders from General Totten in Washington directing him to survey a number of rivers and harbors along the Texas coast. For the first time in his military career, George McClellan would be in charge of his own operation, and he took full advantage of this opportunity. He set up his survey headquarters in Corpus Christi and purchased a small schooner to help his seven-man team complete their survey in a timely manner. His project was completed by March 1853 and his findings were supplied to the officials at Washington. McClellan enjoyed the change of pace, but he would later admit to his sister Maria that, "Although

I am glad to have had it, for the sake of learning something new, yet I must confess that I prefer prairies and pack mules, to the briny and a sail boat."

One unexpected benefit associated with his Texas survey was that it gave Mac an opportunity to renew his acquaintance with an old Mexican War comrade, P. G. T. Beauregard who lived in New Orleans. These men spent many pleasant hours together discussing the science of war and the old times in Mexico. Mac also began to sport a western style mustache at this time. He would keep the mustache for the remainder of his days.

Charles P. Stone

A telegram reached George McClellan on April 7 while he was temporarily stationed at Indianola, Texas. It was sent for the purpose of offering him an opportunity to head up an important exploration project in the great northwest. McClellan would direct the far western half of a survey of the unchartered Cascade Mountain Ridge to help determine the best route for a transcontinental railroad from St. Paul, Minnesota, to Puget Sound. As Mac was preparing to accept the proposed project, an order arrived from General Totten directing him to assume this task. McClellan was ordered to report to Washington to receive additional instructions and to obtain his travel plans.

After receiving his instructions, Mac left New York harbor on May 20, 1853, on the steamer *Illinois* for the Isthmus of Panama. After arriving at his first destination, he made his way to the western coast of Panama and sailed up to the city of San Francisco, a voyage of almost six weeks. He then traveled to Fort Vancouver where he finalized his preparations and organized his equipment. Two men that were employed to help outfit McClellan's team were quartermaster Ulysses S. Grant and Charles P. Stone. McClellan, however, was quite annoyed with Grant because he proved quite unreliable due to his drinking problems. Mac never did forget this incident when Grant was irresponsible in the line of duty.

In spite of minor annoyances and personnel problems, McClellan was glad to be back in command. He was also proud to be among the first non-Indian explorers of the great Cascades. "No one but the Indians knows anything about the country between Mt. Rainier and the boundary," McClellan told his mother. He also asserted, "I shall be pleased as a child with a new toy when I get started. I have a good saddle—a fine command—a new country—hard work and plenty of responsibility on my shoulders—what more could one ask?"

As the survey team began its journey to the Cascades on July 18, 1853, it included sixty-one souls and three months worth of food. The journey was slow and arduous. Most days, the survey team could manage but five miles through the rocky mountain country. After almost eight weeks of exploration, Mac decided to send half of his party, horses and all, back to Fort Vancouver. This would permit his party to travel much faster through the narrow mountain passes. It was with great pleasure that McClellan named one of the most outstanding mountain peaks Mount Stuart, in honor of his dear departed friend.

As Mac neared the end of his survey route, he concluded that he had only found two passes that would possibly be suitable for a railroad. McClellan rendezvoused on October 18 near the Canadian border with the man who commanded the eastern portion of the railroad survey, Governor Stevens. Much to the dismay of McClellan, Stevens proposed that Mac lead his team back through the same mountain passes that they just visited. George McClellan objected to this proposal, for it would involve a dangerous winter excursion that would place tremendous hardships on both men and animals. Although Governor Stevens was not persuaded by Mac's viewpoint, he was unable to force Mac to take this winter excursion. The two men parted company on something less than friendly terms, and Mac lead his team back to the state of Washington, by way of a more southern route.

Several weeks later, Stevens sent a new survey team out under Frederick Lander from Fort Walla Walla to take a fresh look over the mountain passes that were previously studied by McClellan. Needless to say, Mac was deeply offended at what he perceived to be an attack upon his credibility. He refused to give any special assistance to Lander's team and informed Stevens that he would not render additional service to him unless he stopped interfering with his command.

During his final exploration project in January 1854, McClellan and a small party from Puget Sound journeyed to the western region of Yakima Pass. Mac no sooner reached the beginning approach to this pass when he found himself riding through a foot of snow. By this time, McClellan was in no mood to aggressively investigate this mountain pass, and quickly concluded that the snow in the pass must be too deep for rail traffic. This comment was included in the report that was filed with his supervisors and with Governor Stevens. In the final analysis, relations with Mac and Stevens degenerated to the point where much of McClellan's findings were ignored by Stevens.

All in all, the Pacific railroad survey would be relatively inconsequential to McClellan's military career. Further exploration by various parties located four possible routes for the rail line, but no clear consensus could be reached in Congress. The deadlock over which path to take would not be broken until 1862.

When Mac returned to New York in April 1854, a letter from his mother was waiting for him. His mother had recently spent a number of days with the Marcy family and had the opportunity to get to know Miss Nelly Marcy. She wrote, "As to Miss Nelly, she is beautiful…. The young lady has heard so much about you from Captain Marcy that she is just ready to fall in love with you." The letter came at an excellent time, as far as George McClellan was concerned. He soon became anxious to meet the woman who might finally give his life stability. He was plainly tired of drifting through life as a wandering soldier. At age twenty-seven, he longed for romance, family, and a steady dose of home-cooked meals.

In typical McClellan fashion, he sprung into this new "campaign" to win the heart of Ellen (Nelly) Marcy with great enthusiasm. He arranged to meet this young lady in the city of Washington in early May and was not disappointed by what he experienced. On May 14, McClellan felt obliged to write Mrs. Marcy to request permission to court her daughter. He wrote, "The honest truth being that although I have not seen a very great deal of the little lady mentioned above, still that little has been sufficient to make me determined to win her if I can." From the beginning of Mac's offensive to win his sweetheart, he had received nothing but encouragement and support from Mr. and Mrs. Marcy. Now all he needed to do was to get the same encouragement from the young lady named Ellen.

The anxious suitor moved full speed ahead in his courtship of the "little Presbyterian," as he called her. The young lady, however, simply was unable to sense an abiding love in her heart for this qualified bachelor. George McClellan was not going to wait, however, for their relationship to fully blossom—he was on a mission, and he simply must propose to this young woman at once! On a bright morning in June, therefore, McClellan gained a private interview with Miss Nelly and proposed marriage. She flatly rejected his offer. Stunned and heartbroken, McClellan would quickly blame himself for foolishly "pushing too far too quickly." He would have to wait for a better day and pray for the heart of this beautiful woman to soften towards him.

In the midst of his mourning, Mac received orders from the Secretary of War, Jefferson Davis, that would quickly send him away from his embarrassing trials for the summer. McClellan set sail on June 28, 1854, aboard the frigate *Columbia*. He was being sent on a secret assignment to the Dominican Republic to evaluate their anchorage and coaling station to see if it was suitable for the navy's use. Jefferson Davis was interested in determining whether it was feasible for the United States to establish a military base in the Dominican Republic.

McClellan spent almost two months surveying the military and civilian installations on this small island before sailing back to the city of Washington. He filed a detailed report with the Secretary of War regarding his findings, and was relieved to tell Mrs. Marcy that, "The Secretary expressed himself as being very much pleased with the result of my summer's work, and the manner in which it had been conducted." One month later, Jefferson Davis directed McClellan to perform a detailed report on the nation's established railroads in regard to their maintenance and construction costs. This project greatly enhanced Mac's understanding of railroad engineering and operational policies "a new pursuit to me," he wrote, "should I ever desire to leave the army."

Jefferson Davis

Just when George McClellan was beginning to seriously think about resigning from the military, he received his long overdue promotion to the rank of Captain on March 3, 1855. This turn of events, coupled with the interest that Jefferson Davis was showing in his career, encouraged Mac to keep his commission. A short time later, the Secretary of War appointed Captain McClellan to be part of a three member commission to study the latest military developments in Europe. McClellan would soon sail to Europe with two senior officers in a year-long fact finding tour. One special aspect of their trip would be to personally observe the war that was then raging in the Crimea.

"McClellan would soon sail to Europe...."

Needless to say, the well-publicized tour was the opportunity of a lifetime for so young an officer as George McClellan. Before he set sail on April 11, he wrote, "Of course I feel much flattered by the choice."

In addition to visiting numerous battlefields in the Crimea, McClellan and his companions toured most of the capitals of Europe and visited with many heads of State. During his tour, Captain McClellan collected over 100 books and military manuals covering everything from cavalry tactics to veterinary medicine. When McClellan returned home in late April 1856, he was able to be stationed in Philadelphia. He was granted permission to stay in his mother's house while he completed his detailed reports about current military trends in Europe.

Due to Captain McClellan's extensive knowledge of foreign languages, he was able to easily translate the French and German military manuals in his possession. When it came to working with the Russian text, he simply decided to teach himself the Russian language. Less than three months later, he completed the translation of a three-hundred page Russian cavalry manual. The army would eventually adopt and publish the Russian cavalry manual translated by George McClellan.

Another interesting result of Mac's trip to Europe was that it gave him the opportunity to design and patent a military-style saddle not unlike those that were used in the Hungarian cavalry during this period. The saddle also contained special modifications found useful in other cavalry units across Europe. The United States army adopted the "McClellan saddle" in the late 1850s and it remained the standard issue saddle for as long as the U.S. military utilized horse cavalry.

The military commission report that was presented by McClellan would firmly establish his reputation as an expert of war tactics. It is more than ironic, however, that at a time when McClellan's military star was finally beginning to rise that he decided to resign. Many historians speculate that McClellan's departure at this time was due, at least in part, to his unwillingness to endure the slow pace of peacetime promotions. Captain McClellan resigned his commission on January 15, 1857, at the age of thirty. He would now try to find his happiness in civilian life and hopefully find a wife in the process.

Chapter Five

The Railroad Man

1857–1860

While George McClellan was finishing up his military commission report during the last half of 1856, he was also hunting for a job in the civilian marketplace. Through the help of an old army buddy, G. W. Smith and a wealthy New York lawyer named Samuel Barlow, McClellan secured a job as chief engineer for the Illinois Central Railroad. Mac started with the railroad in late January 1857 and moved to their central office in Chicago. Just one year after joining this company, engineer Mac was promoted to the position of vice-president of the railroad.

When George McClellan was not occupied with his inspection tours of the railroad line, he would relax with a cigar at the Chicago Light Guard militia headquarters or write his friend Miss Ellen Marcy. Even though Mac was a successful business executive with a maid and personal chef, he knew that something was still missing. George wrote to his friend, Ellen during this time confessing his loneliness:

> Can't you find among your acquaintances some quiet young woman of a moral turn of mind, who can sew on buttons, look happy when I come home, drive off my neuralgia, and make herself generally useful (including going to the market) who will come out on speculation...?

Quite naturally, McClellan missed the companionship of his military friends, almost as much as he did the companionship of a wife. He was barely in Chicago six months before he began to investigate the possibility of rejoining the military ranks. Mac watched the papers with interest as they wrote about the growing crisis in the Utah territory with the Mormons. Late in 1857, McClellan traveled to Washington for the express purpose of lobbying for the right to command one of the regiments that would be sent to suppress the Mormon rebellion.

During this same year, Mac would also be preoccupied with a serious financial crisis that affected his railroad called the Panic of 1857. A panic in the stock market caused many banks and security firms to close and caused general unrest in the economy. The administrative skills of George McClellan were put to the test during this crisis. He was under constant pressure to cut costs, lay off workers, and scale back operations in general. Unlike many railroads during this time, the Illinois Central Company was saved from bankruptcy due to the wise and level headed leadership of McClellan. By the end of 1858, the Illinois Central had weathered the financial storm and was able to resume dividend payments to its shareholders.

Mr. G. W. Smith, an old friend of McClellan, informed him that the board of directors was most unhappy with the prospect of his resigning from the railroad. They felt that the railroad needed a stable leadership base to reassure the public and the stockholders that their company was indeed moving forward. McClellan responded to this revelation by expressing his true sentiments to businessman and friend, Samuel Barlow:

> Railroading is all very well… but I like the old business better and if you can get me back into the service, I trust I do not flatter myself, when I say that you will make a pretty good soldier out of a bad railroad man…. Life is too short to waste bickering about cross ties and contracts—I cannot learn to love it. In God's name, give me all the help you can—I should die out here in another year.

Another factor in George McClellan's renewed interest in military life was due to the exploits of his former commander and friend, Randolph Marcy. In March 1858, Marcy led a thrilling rescue mission during the dead of winter to resupply three army regiments who were trapped in Utah. This expedition, which drew national attention, did much to rekindle his desire to put on the uniform of his country once again. For better or for worse, however, the mili-

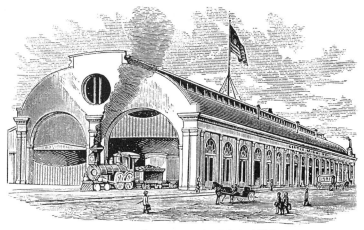

Railroad Station in the Mid–1800s

tary confrontation with the Mormons remained bloodless and slowly faded away. As a consequence, the military officials at Washington elected not to enlist McClellan's support. He would have to settle for being a successful and wealthy businessman for at least a while longer.

Even though the railroad business was not a tremendous thrill to George McClellan, it certainly had its benefits. His steady income permitted him to purchase a large home on Chicago's lakefront. He generously agreed to share his home with an old West Point friend named Ambrose Burnside, who came to him in search of employment after having gone bankrupt. Mac not only opened his home to this gentleman and his wife, but found a position for "Burn" at the railroad. These men would become best friends as the years passed and would both become Union generals during the War Between the States.

McClellan also had the opportunity to become acquainted with a private detective named Allan Pinkerton who was under contract with the railroad to protect their property. This detective would eventually become active with the Union Army during the Civil War as a secret service or intelligence officer. As a general in the Union Army, McClellan would rely heavily upon the information gathered by Pinkerton's men. During Mac's railroad days, he also came into contact with a middle-aged lawyer from Springfield named Abraham Lincoln who handled several legal cases for the Illinois Central. For the most part, George McClellan was unimpressed with the lanky lawyer named Lincoln. The indifference that Mac felt may have been driven by the fact that the two men walked in very different social and political realms.

Ambrose Powell Hill

George McClellan was a strong supporter of the conservative Democratic cause and openly supported Stephen A. Douglas in his 1858 bid for the senatorial seat in Illinois. As you may guess, Douglas ran against Lincoln during this political contest. On one occasion, if not more, Mac loaned Douglas his private train car to travel to political events throughout Illinois. George McClellan recorded in his memoirs how he actually escorted Douglas to the location of one of his famous debates with Abraham Lincoln. During the debate, McClellan wrote, "Douglas's speech was compact, logical and powerful—Mr. Lincoln's disjointed, and rather a mass of anecdotes than of arguments. I did not think that there was any approach to equality in the oratorical powers of the two men." Not surprisingly, conservative George voted with Douglas during the campaign.

While Mac was keeping busy climbing up the corporate ladder, his long lost love, Ellen Marcy, was keeping more than busy trying to juggle her long list of would be husbands. By the middle of 1859, Ellen had received nine proposals for marriage, including the disastrous overture by McClellan some years before. One of these proposals, by West Point graduate Ambrose Powell Hill, was actually accepted by Ellen Marcy during 1856 only to be later nullified by parental disapproval. It would take a strange twist of Providence to turn the "let's be friends and pen pals" relationship that existed between Mac and Ellen Marcy into a genuine love relationship.

A few months later, October 1859 to be exact, the hand of Providence did indeed bring the estranged couple into close contact once again. Ellen's dad, Randolph Marcy, was transferred to a new post at St. Paul, Minnesota, and he decided to take his family with him. As soon as Mac heard the news, he sent off an invitation for the Marcys to stay at his home a few days while they traveled through the Chicago area. Robert

Ellen Marcy and Mac

Marcy had not seen McClellan in years, but they had kept in touch by mail. The fact that McClellan had left the service had only increased his suitability for marriage in the eyes of Mr. Marcy. This fact was shared with Ellen on more than one occasion. At any event, the Marcys were glad to have received McClellan's invitation and would plan to stop in Chicago for a short visit.

When Ellen Marcy stepped down from the train on October 20, she noticed a very different George McClellan. He was more dignified and more mature in his new role as a prominent businessman with a mansion on Lake Michigan. It was also obvious to Ellen that one thing had not changed about old George, he still loved her intensely. He had never really loved anyone beside his dear Nelly.

Four days later, after a pleasant round of talks and walks, the Marcy family boarded Mac's private rail car bound for St. Paul. This time, however, George climbed aboard himself and continued the courtship of Miss Nelly. He was not going to let her get away, not now, or ever. In less than 48 hours, on the way to St. Paul, George McClellan sought to unite himself to Ellen Marcy once again. He proposed and she accepted, with the full approval of her loving parents! It was, indeed a miracle of God's grace that this couple could be united in Christian love.

The news of their engagement could hardly be described as shocking, but it was nevertheless received enthusiastically by virtually all. George McClellan's mother, who always had possessed the utmost respect for little Nelly, wrote her an encouraging letter stating in part: "Dear Miss Nelly, I know Mary and I need not now offer great protestations of affections, for, from the earliest times of our acquaintance, our hearts warmed to you, and you have ever since been thought and spoken of by us both, as one to be dearly loved."

As George McClellan returned to Chicago, he determined to write daily to his betrothed during the seven months of their engagement. Many of the letters that Mac wrote his bride were preserved and reveal a tremendous spiritual change in McClellan's view of life.

As McClellan contemplated marriage and life in general, he truly experienced a substantial evangelical regeneration that dramatically affected his worldview. From the days of his youth, Mac knew Jesus Christ to be the Savior. Now, for the first time, perhaps, he knew Jesus to be his personal Savior and Lord. God used the influence of Ellen Marcy to deepen his commitment to the Christian faith. Mac soon began to embrace a Bible-centered or Calvinistic view of faith. It was a faith that acknowledged the total sovereign control of Christ over every individual, nation, and event of history. No longer would George feel hopeless or indulge a pessimistic view of the future. His times, and Ellen's as well, were understood to be in God's Almighty hands—and that was just where he wanted them to be.

The wedding was held at Calvary Protestant Episcopal Church in New York City on May 22, 1860. The minister who performed the service was Rev. Francis H. Hawks. He was joined by a host of high profile witnesses which included General Winfield Scott, a former governor of Connecticut, Joseph E. Johnston, and of course, A. P. Hill. After the reception, the happy couple boarded the train for Chicago. McClellan would later write that his wedding day was the best day of his life. He wrote his mother in the spirit of marital bliss with this encouraging news, "You can scarcely imagine how changed everything seems to me now.... I believe I am the happiest man that ever lived and am sure that I have the dearest wife in all the world." After twenty-five years of marriage, George McClellan would still be able to joyfully echo these words.

In August 1860, Mac decided to take advantage of a new position that was offered to him by longtime friend and railroad tycoon, Samuel Barlow. George and Nelly moved from Chicago to Cincinnati as George began to assume his new position as the President of the eastern division of the Ohio and Mississippi Railroad. Mac rented a comfortable home in Cincinnati and was soon enjoying the challenges of a new job in a new city. As usual, McClellan soon made his share of enemies at the railroad by what he termed his "naturally defiant disposition." The childish habit of becoming obstinate in the face of criticism or opposition would continue to plague Mac during most of his adult life, although he did make noticeable progress over this character flaw after his conversion to Christ.

Ellen and George McClellan would only be blessed with slightly under one year together before the ugly spectacle of war would temporarily disrupt their happy home. With the recent election of Abraham Lincoln to the office of President, the sectional conflict deepened throughout the United States. George watched with disgust as the state of South Carolina seceded from the Union in late 1860. He also noted how the extremists in New England shamelessly fanned the flames of hatred and distrust in an effort to shame the South into abandoning its position on slavery and state sovereignty. Mac wrote his brother-in-law who lived in Alabama stating that he was still mildly optimistic that a political compromise could be worked out between the North and the South. He felt that the only possible way to avoid civil war was to somehow neutralize the fanatical "ultras" among the abolitionists and the secessionist crowds. McClellan took the threat of civil war seriously enough to build a clause into his home's rental agreement that would "release me from the obligation in the event of war." George McClellan would always remain convinced that extremists in the North and South were responsible for the bloody tragedy known as the War Between the States.

Notwithstanding McClellan's view of who started the war and why, when push came to shove, Mac would cast his lot with the Union. In mid-April, when the South Carolina military fired on federally controlled Fort Sumter in Charleston Harbor, McClellan told his longtime friend Fitz John Porter, "I throw to one side now all questions as to the past—political parties, etc.,...—the government is in danger, our flag insulted, and we must stand by it."

Fort Sumter

For a change, Mac would not have to go out looking for a military command. As one who was considered "chock full of big war science," George Brinton McClellan would soon have his pick of choice military positions within the Union army.

Chapter Six

A Call to Arms

1861

When Fort Sumter surrendered to the Confederate forces in South Carolina during April 1861, George McClellan was enjoying a prosperous career and a happy home life in Cincinnati. Few railroad administrators in the country could boast a larger salary than McClellan. His annual salary was $10,000, which was a significant sum for this period.

In addition to his financial and domestic blessings, George McClellan could hardly have relished the thought of waging war against many of his old classmates and comrades in the South. Mac, for instance was already aware of the fact that his good friend from New Orleans, P. G. T. Beauregard, had recently been commissioned a general in the Confederate army. It was Beauregard who directed the South Carolina forces against the Federal troops stationed at Fort Sumter. Nevertheless, in spite of old friendships, wealth, and domestic tranquillity, Mac would not hesitate to pick up his sword.

For a patriot like George McClellan, there never was any question as to whether he would forsake worldly pleasure for the sake of his country. Like millions of Americans, North and South, he would willingly risk his life and fortune because he was convicted that the honor of his country was at stake. In McClellan's case, he also possessed a sincere personal conviction that he was called of God to save the Union, and with it, Christian civil order in North America.

During the opening days of the war, McClellan received official contacts from the states of Pennsylvania, New York, and Ohio requesting him to take command of their state militias. Although Mac had a difficult time choosing between these three posts, he soon took the position of major general of the Ohio volunteers. Within a matter of days, General McClellan also received a commission in the regular army from General Winfield Scott in Washington which confirmed him as major general of the Department of the Ohio. This command eventually included about 20,000 volunteers from the states of Ohio, Indiana, Illinois, far-western Pennsylvania, and a large portion of western Virginia.

On April 15, Abraham Lincoln called for a volunteer force of 75,000 men to invade the Southern States in the hopes of putting a quick end to the Confederacy. This act caused four more southern states, including Virginia, to secede from the Union. It was President Lincoln who determined to make his stand at Fort Sumter and insisted that this Federal fort be resupplied, if necessary, by force. For better or worse, the

Major General McClellan

Confederate forces "took the bait" and forced the Federal troops to evacuate Fort Sumter in Charleston Harbor. The firing on Fort Sumter began one of the saddest chapters in American history, as Americans would soon be killing each other wholesale.

Not surprisingly, the incident at Fort Sumter and the actions of the Lincoln administration soon turned the peaceful states into great camps preparing for war. General McClellan worked closely with the governor of Ohio and the War Department in Washington in an attempt to mobilize, equip, and train the thousands of Union soldiers that would be needed to defeat the Confederate forces. One of the chief difficulties that McClellan faced during this period of organization stemmed from the fact that many of the experienced officers in the regular army had enlisted in the Confederate cause.

Consequently, General McClellan would not be able to secure the support of skilled soldiers like Robert E. Lee, Joseph Johnson, James Longstreet, A. P. Hill, and P. G. T. Beauregard. This fact made it doubly difficult for General McClellan to quickly and adequately prepare his volunteers for combat duty.

The newly appointed head of the Department of the Ohio, George McClellan, would also soon learn of the pathetic condition of the state armories. McClellan inspected the military equipment and arms that were in storage in the Ohio armories and found little more than a few tired cannons and piles of worn-out rifles and field gear. As a result, Major-general McClellan sent a detailed requisition to Washington for thousands of new uniforms, cannons, rifles, and tents. Slowly but surely, the equipment of war began to stream into the new military camps that were established in Ohio by General McClellan.

As any experienced commander can testify, it takes more than good equipment and arms to make a successful army. George McClellan, in particular, was keenly aware that his mob of new recruits needed a steady dose of good discipline and training before they would be prepared for battle. McClellan wrote his first general order to his new volunteer soldiers from the city of Columbus, Ohio on April 25, 1861, stating the following:

> *To Ohio Volunteer Militia*
>
> *General Order, Head Quarters, Ohio Volunteer Militia*
> *No. 1[Columbus] April 25th, 1861*
>
> *By the direction of the Governor of Ohio, the undersigned hereby assumes command of the Ohio Volunteer Militia mustered into the service of the United States.*
>
> *In doing so, he desires to call the attention of the officers and men to the fact, that discipline and instruction are of as much importance in war as mere courage. He asks for and expects the cheerful cooperation of the entire command in his efforts to establish discipline and efficiency, the surest guarantees of success.*
>
> *Until the organization is perfected, many inconveniences must be*

endured, for the sudden [urgency], which has made it necessary to call so largely upon your patriotism, has rendered it impossible for the authorities to make, in an instant, the requisite preparation.

We do not enter upon this war as a pastime, but with the stern determination to repel the insults offered to our flag, and uphold the honor and integrity of our Union.

In the coming struggle, we have not only battles to fight, but hardships and privations to endure, fatigue to encounter.

The General Commanding does not doubt, that the spirit which has prompted you to leave your homes and those most dear to you, will support you firmly in the future.

He asks your willing obedience and full confidence—having obtained that, he feels sure that he can conduct you to glory, and to victories that will ensure safety to your homes and lasting response to the country.

Geo. B. McClellan
Major General O.V.M.

It was the intention of General McClellan to secure every advantage for his growing army, and it was in that spirit that he secretly sent a letter to the Chicago based private detective, Allan Pinkerton. McClellan wrote:

To Allan Pinkerton

Allan Pinkerton, Esq.

Dear Sir:—Columbus, Ohio, April 24, 1861.

I wish to see you with the least possible delay, to make arrangements with you of an important nature. I will be either here or in Cincinnati for the next few days—here to-morrow—Cincinnati next day. In this city you will find me at the Capitol, at Cincinnati at my residence. If you telegraph me, better use your first name alone. Let no one know that you come to see me, and keep as quiet as possible.

Very truly yours,

Geo. B. McClellan
Maj. Gen'l Comd'g Ohio Vols.

Allan Pinkerton, President Lincoln, and General John A. McClernand

The reason for the secrecy was that McClellan was poised to offer Pinkerton the directorship of his intelligence-gathering operations. Mac well understood the importance of good military intelligence to his future command strategies. For obvious reasons, the general did not wish to reveal his intentions to utilize the services of this well-known detective for fear it would compromise his future effectiveness as a spy. As the war expanded, General McClellan would eventually permit Pinkerton to run a vast intelligence agency and spy ring in an effort to obtain important military intelligence such as southern troops strengths and proposed battle plans.

As it turned out, the confidence that McClellan placed in Pinkerton's intelligence work was consistently misplaced and extremely damaging to his efforts as a field commander. Pinkerton consistently estimated Confederate troop strengths at twice their actual size. This misleading intelligence caused McClellan to approach every battle with undue caution and ultimately gained him the undeserved reputation of being an indecisive bumbler.

While General McClellan sought to put together an effective intelligence team, he continued to oversee the training and equipping of his troops. As McClellan prepared to move his headquarters to the city of Cincinnati, he brought Major Randolph Marcy into

his administrative circle as paymaster and chief-of-staff. Major
Marcy provided McClellan with a great deal of assistance and moral
support during his turbulent period as a Union general.

By the end of May 1861, McClellan was in a position to send a
few of his better trained and equipped volunteer regiments against
the small Confederate forces that occupied western Virginia. A brief
skirmish was fought at the tiny town of Philippi on June 3 and
resulted in the total route of the Confederate positions. Six hundred
ill-equipped Confederate soldiers fled their emplacements in Philippi and ran away from the Union troops shortly after the opening
volley of cannon fire. These unseasoned Southerners were apparently disinterested in facing cannons and modern rifles with little
more than old flint-lock pistols and rusty muskets. When the news
of this engagement reached General McClellan in Cincinnati, he
was pleased to hear about the Confederate route known as the
"Philippi Races." This was the first land battle of the war and the
first victory for General McClellan.

Although the news of this first Union victory sent smiles across
the faces of many in Washington, it was far less appreciated in Richmond. General Robert E. Lee sent his own adjutant, Brigadier General Robert S. Garnett to reorganize and reinvigorate the
Confederate forces in western Virginia. The Southern cause would
be greatly hindered if western Virginia fell under the control of
Union forces, and Lee was determined to fight when and where he
could.

On June 14, the stern General Garnett reached the mountain
regions of Virginia. He quickly split his forces into two separate regiments. One of these regiments, consisting of about 1,000 men, was
sent to a key mountain pass on the western edge of Rich Mountain.
The remaining troops, about 4,000 in all, were sent to confront the
Union garrison at Philippi. The Confederate forces under Garnett
slowly moved into their positions and were dug in by June 20th.

The same day that Garnett's troops dug in around Philippi and
Rich Mountain, McClellan decided that it was time for him to

travel by train to the mountains of western Virginia. On June 20, Mac kissed his wife Nelly good-by and headed for the battlefield.

A few days later, Nelly, who was six months pregnant, received a letter from her husband describing how his journey to the front was "one continual ovation all along the road and at every station where we stopped." He went on to add, "crowds had assembled to see the 'Young Napoleon'. Gray-headed old men and women; mothers holding up their children to take my hand, girls, boys, all sorts, cheering and crying, God bless you! I never went through such a scene in my life and never expect to go through such another one."

On June 25, 1861, Major General McClellan wrote his men upon arriving at his new field headquarters at Grafton, Virginia. He reminded his troops to...

> Bear in mind that you are in the country of friends, not of enemies; that you are here to protect, not to destroy. Take nothing, destroy nothing, unless you are ordered to do so by your General officers. Remember that I have pledged my word to the people of Western Virginia, that their rights in person and property shall be respected. I ask every one of you to make good this promise in its broadest sense. We come here to save, not to upturn. I do not appeal to the fear of punishment, but to your appreciation of the sacredness of the cause in which we are engaged. Carry with you into battle the conviction that you are right, and that God is on your side.

> Your enemies have violated every moral law—neither God nor man can sustain them. They have without cause rebelled against a mild and paternal Government; they have seized upon public and private property; they have outraged the persons of Northern men merely because they loved the Union; they have placed themselves beneath contempt, unless they can retrieve some honor on the field of battle. You will pursue a different course. You will be honest, brave, and merciful; you will respect the right of private opinion; you will punish no man for opinion's sake. Show to the world that you differ from our enemies in the points of honor, honesty and respect for private opinion, and that we inaugurate no reign of terror where we go.

Soldiers! I have heard that there was danger here. I fear now but one thing—that you will not find foemen worthy of your steel. I know that I can rely upon you.

Geo. B. McClellan
Major Gen'l Commanding

As the days of early July dawned upon the Union forces, McClellan was busy making final preparations for his offensive against the Confederate forces. He issued his plans to his field commanders, which included an attack with seven thousand soldiers and light artillery against the enemy that was dug in around Rich Mountain. His major objectives were to route the enemy at Rich Mountain while pressing on to occupy the town of Beverly which was located in the rear of the Confederate forces under Garnett. This plan was intended to cut off and entrap the entire force of Confederates in western Virginia. McClellan was confident that he could defeat the enemy if he could catch them in his "net." "I expect to thrash the infamous scamps before a week is over—all I fear is that I can't catch them!" exclaimed the young Union general.

As McClellan moved his troops into position, he wrote his wife a letter on July 5 that revealed his understandable nervousness. He wrote, "I realize now the dreadful responsibility on me—the lives of my men—the reputation of my country and the success of our cause.... I shall feel my way and be very cautious, for I recognize the fact that everything requires success in my first operations. You need not be at all alarmed as to the result—God is on our side."

On July 11, McClellan sent a brigade of infantry under the command of General Rosecrans to the enemy's left flank around Rich Mountain. As soon as Rosecrans men engaged the Confederate troops lead by Colonel John Pegram, the noise of battle would signal McClellan to attack with two brigades in the enemy's front. Heavy rains, however, delayed the assault lead by General Rosecrans and also lead to a great deal of confusion as McClellan was only able to receive sporadic reports from the field. As a consequence, the frontal assault planned by McClellan was postponed until July 12. News from the fighting around Rich Mountain finally reached the camp of Commander McClellan and was, in fact, better than expected.

The success of Rosecrans's engagement on the Confederate's left flank was nearly complete and the enemy was in disarray. By July 13, the battered Confederates under Colonel Pegram forwarded a message to General McClellan which announced their willingness to surrender. Two-thirds of Pegram's original force of 1,300, including 600 officers, were either killed or eventually surrendered. When news of the rout reached the Confederate commander Garnett, who was with his forces at Laurel Hill several miles away, he immediately gave orders for his men to evacuate their positions. Garnett knew that a speedy retreat was the only opportunity that his troops had to avoid being entrapped and destroyed.

As the Confederates began to retreat, McClellan ordered a brigade under General Morris to pursue the enemy in the hopes of destroying at least a portion of their forces. A sharp skirmish was fought on July 13 between the Union forces and the rear guard of General Garnett's men. During this brief but bloody engagement, General Garnett fell mortally wounded as he sought to rally his beleaguered host.

The following day, McClellan telegraphed Washington to inform General Winfield Scott of the good news that "Our success is complete and secession is killed in this country." Efforts were naturally made by McClellan's men to cut-off the main body of Garnett's forces before they could reach the safety of the Shenandoah Valley. Poor coordination and general inexperience, however, caused the final offensive against the retreating Confederates to be largely ineffective. General Robert E. Lee would lose the western part of Virginia to the Union forces, but would salvage a great number of the troops and equipment that were sent into this region. This fact, in Lee's view, was but a small consolation in light of the military and political implications resulting from the loss of a portion of his beloved Virginia. Lee himself would make one last attempt in late July 1861, to reclaim western Virginia. His efforts, however, would not be any more effectual that those of his predecessor. In less than

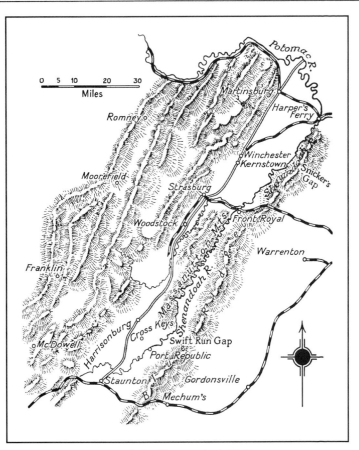

Map of the Shenandoah Valley

two years, the pro-Union minded people of western Virginia would separate to become the new state of West Virginia.

Almost overnight, the thirty-four year old general from Philadelphia, George Brinton McClellan, had become the first genuine hero of the Union army. The North was hungry for good news from the battlefield, and the small but strategic victory that McClellan's forces obtained in western Virginia was received with great enthusiasm— even euphoria. The United States Congress passed a joint resolution that expressed the thankfulness of the nation for the military achievements of George McClellan and his army.

President Lincoln was clearly pleased with the reports of this victory that were personally dropped off to him by Major Randolph Marcy. A number of Confederate battle flags were also presented to the President which were captured during the fighting in Virginia. Randolph Marcy also paid a visit to the general-in-chief Winfield Scott, informing him of the desire that McClellan had to make "a movement through Kentucky, Western Tennessee and Northern Alabama which would be decisive of the war." As General Scott and President Lincoln contemplated their next military offensive against the South, which they hoped would bring the war to a swift close, the Confederate army was preparing to meet them with great determination.

In the middle of July 1861, McClellan received a communication from Winfield Scott which outlined a plan for the next major, and he hoped, decisive battle. This plan called for McClellan to move east into the Shenandoah Valley so as to combine forces with General Robert Patterson's troops for an all out attack upon the Confederate forces under Joe Johnston. During the same time frame, a large Union army under the command of Irving McDowell would leave their camp at Washington and march twenty-five miles to attack the Southern forces at Manassas Junction.

This plan, and the naive optimism that prompted it, would soon be smashed by the clever maneuverings of Mac's old friends P. G. T. Beauregard and Joseph Johnston. While McDowell's army moved toward Manassas Junction on July 20, General Joe Johnston quietly moved most of his army from the Shenandoah Valley to join his forces with General Beauregard who was stationed at Manassas. As a consequence, the combined Confederate forces would be ready to meet the attack of the Union army under McDowell.

The confident Union army attacked the Confederate forces who were dug in along an area known as Bull Run. The first wave of infantry managed to press the Confederates all along the line during the morning of July 21. At many points on the battlefield, the Southerners were beginning to loose ground and General Beauregard feared that his men would break and run. Suddenly, at a strategic point in the Confederate line, an experienced line officer named Thomas J. Jackson appeared out of the smoke to call for his brigade to stand fast. This brigade responded to the call and charged upon the exposed Union troops with bayonets and wild cheers. Minutes later, the reinforcements commanded by Joseph Johnston arrived on the battlefield and began to charge upon the Union line with reckless abandon. By day's end, the entire army under McDowell was in full retreat back to Washington. Hundreds of valuable rifles and several cannons fell into the hands of the victorious Confederates, along with vast amounts of food and equipment.

The battle of Bull Run or First Manassas totally demoralized the Northern army. For days after the battle, thousands of Union soldiers slowly made their way back to their capital at Washington. The bright hopes of Union victory and a quick end to the war were forever dashed in pieces. On the other hand, the South was elated at this turn of events. The Battle of Bull Run would create a host of heroes within the Confederacy. It would establish Thomas J. Jackson in particular as a genuine military hero and earn him the name of "Stonewall" for his courageous stand before the charging enemy.

The Union Secretary of War Cameron found it convenient to blame most of the defeat at Bull Run upon General McDowell who was quickly released from command. The North required a new leader who could reorganize their broken army. A telegram was sent on July 22 to the only man who was considered qualified to rebuild the Union forces surrounding Washington, and that man was none other than George Brinton McClellan. The telegram received by Mac at the town of Beverly read, "Circumstances make your presence here necessary. Charge Rosecrans or some other general with your present department and come hither without delay."

While General McClellan sped his way toward Washington, the capital was already bracing for what many Northern leaders felt was a probable attack by the Confederates. Pure chaos reigned in the once peaceful city of Washington as leaders throughout the North prayed for someone to come and set things in order.

Chapter Seven

Highly Exalted

1861–1862

On July 26, a military train deposited General George McClellan in the city of Washington. He immediately scheduled a meeting with Winfield Scott to obtain a clearer idea of the condition of things in the capital. The next morning, McClellan was directed by the adjutant general to call upon the President for a high level meeting.

The meeting between Lincoln and Mac was cordial in every respect and was something of a reunion. General McClellan included the following remarks in his memoirs regarding this special conference with President Lincoln:

> Long before the war, when vice-president of the Illinois Central Railroad Company, I knew Mr. Lincoln, for he was one of the counsel of the company. More than once I have been with him in out-of-the-way county seats where some important case was being tried and, in the lack of sleeping accommodations, have spent the night in front of a stove listening to the unceasing flow of anecdotes from his lips. He was never at a loss, and I could never quite make up my mind how many of them he had really heard before, and how many he invented on the spur of the moment. His stories were seldom refined, but were always to the point.

The morning meeting with Lincoln included few surprises for the expectant young general from Philadelphia. He was placed in command of the military forces in and around Washington. Later in the day, Mac again visited the office of General Scott who directed him to take a ride around Washington to see the condition of the regiments first hand. McClellan wrote his wife to explain what he saw during this brief inspection of his troops. He wrote,

After leaving the general I rode around the outskirts of the city on the Maryland side towards Tennallytown, Seventh Street, etc., and examined some of the camps, but did not devote myself individually to the police work of picking up drunken stragglers. I found no preparations whatever for defense.... Not a regiment was properly encamped, not a single avenue of approach guarded. All was chaos, and the streets, hotels, and barrooms were filled with drunken officers and men absent from their regiments without leave—a

General Winfield Scott

perfect pandemonium.

General McClellan meet briefly with President Lincoln and his cabinet the next day and then plunged right into his enormous duties and responsibilities. From the very first day, he energetically took command of what became known as the Army of the Potomac. The young Napoleon exhibited immense organizational and administrative talent. What's more, he used his personal charm and charisma to gain almost universal support from the influential and powerful in Washington. At the close of July 1861, McClellan informed his wife of the amazing set of circumstances that surrounded him. He remarked with an air of surprise that...

> President, Cabinet, General Scott, and all are deferring to me—by some strange operation of magic. I seem to have become the power of the Land. I almost think that were I to win some small success now I could become Dictator or anything else that might please me—but nothing of that kind would please me—therefore I won't be Dictator. Admirable self-denial!

While Mac continued to busy himself with reorganizing and reequipping the forces around Washington, his relationship with General-in-Chief Scott quickly began to deteriorate. During the frequent meetings that McClellan had with Lincoln and his cabinet, he often found himself in profound disagreement with the ideas of the general-in-chief. Mac wrote to his wife, Ellen, stating, "The old general always comes in the way. He understands nothing, appreciates nothing.... I have to fight my way against him.... Our ideas are so widely different that it is impossible for us to work together much longer." Much to the disappointment of George McClellan, his relationship continued to decline with the aged Winfield Scott. On August 9, Mac wrote to his wife again to describe his busy and often frustrating life in Washington. The letter appears below:

To Mary Ellen McClellan

Washington Aug 9 [10] 1861 1 A.M.

I have had a busy day—started from here at 7 in the morning & was in the saddle until about 9 this evening [August 9]—rode over the advanced positions on the other side of the river, was soundly drenched in a hard rain & have been busy ever since my return. Things are improving daily—I received 3 new rgts today—fitted out one new battery yesterday, another today—two tomorrow—about five day after. Within four days I hope to have at least 21 batteries—say 124 field guns—18 co's. of cavalry & some 70 rgts of infantry. Gen'l Scott is the great obstacle—he will not comprehend the danger & is either a traitor or an incompetent. I have to fight my way against him & have thrown a bombshell that has created a perfect stampeded in the Cabinet— tomorrow [August 10] the question will probably be decided by giving me absolute control independently of him. I suppose it will result in a mortal enmity on his part against me, but I have no choice—the people call upon me to save the country—I must save it & cannot respect anything that is in the way.

I receive letter after letter—have conversation after conversation calling on me to save the nation—alluding to the Presidency, Dictatorship &c. As I hope one day to be united with you forever in heaven, I have no such aspirations—I will never accept the Presidency—I will cheerfully take the Dictatorship and agree to lay down my life when the country is saved. I am not spoiled by my unexpected & new position—I feel sure that God will give me the strength & wisdom to preserve this great nation—but I tell you, who share all my thoughts, that I have no selfish feeling in the matter. I feel that God has placed a great work in my hands—I have not sought it—I know how weak I am—but I know that I mean to do right & I believe that God will help me & give me the wisdom I do not possess. Pray for me, darling, that I may be able to accomplish my task—the greatest, perhaps, that any poor weak mortal ever had to do....

God grant that I may bring this war to an end & be permitted to spend the rest of my days quietly with you....

As one might expect, George McClellan did not continue to enjoy the same level of cooperation that embraced him when he arrived in Washington. Many senior military officers like Winfield Scott had a difficult time hiding their natural resentment for the special attention and privileges that were being showered upon the thirty-four year old upstart general named McClellan. At this stage, however, McClellan's relationship with the President and most of his cabinet was still rather good. Although Lincoln was a Republican and Mac a Democrat, they shared a common view of the limited purpose or aims of the Civil War. Neither man wished to do anything other than end the war by bringing the South back into the Union of States. They both consistently rejected the radical abolitionist aim of fighting to bring the South to its knees so as to force them to instantly abandon slavery. These men believed that once the Confederate states re-entered the Union, the slavery issue could proceed to be gradually resolved in the halls of Congress.

When Abraham Lincoln was campaigning for the Presidency, he made it clear that although he opposed slavery in principle, he would only act to stop its expansion into the territories. Lincoln's inauguration speech in March 1861, contained this viewpoint, "I have no purpose, directly or indirectly, to interfere with the institution of slavery in the states where it exists. I believe I have no lawful right to do so, and I have no inclination to do so." Like most politicians of this era, Lincoln perceived the issue of slavery to be as dangerous as a minefield. As a result, he avoided trying to tackle the problem of slavery in a straight forward fashion.

Shortly after George McClellan came to Washington, he was confronted by influential abolitionists who interrogated him regarding his view of the slavery issue. McClellan left a record of one particular conversation that he had in this regard with Senator Charles Sumner. Mac stated:

> Soon after my arrival in Washington… I had several interviews with prominent abolitionists—of whom Senator [Charles] Sumner was one—on the subject of slavery. I invariably took the ground that I was thoroughly opposed to slavery, regarding it as a great evil… but that in my opinion no sweeping measure of emancipation should be carried out unless accompanied by arrangements providing for the new relations between employers and employed, carefully guarding the rights and interests of both…. Mr. Sumner

replied—others also agreed with him—that such points did not concern us, and that all of that must be left to take care of itself.

My reply was that no real statesman could ever contemplate so sweeping and serious a measure as sudden and general emancipation without looking to the future and providing for its consequences; that four and a half millions of uneducated slaves should not suddenly be manumitted without due precautions taken both to protect them and to guard against them.... My own view was that emancipation should be accomplished gradually, and that the Negroes should be fitted for it by certain preparatory steps in the way of education, recognition of the rights of family and marriage, prohibition against selling them without their own consent, the freedom of those born after a certain date, etc....

I recognized the fact that as the Confederate States had chosen to resort to the arbitrament of arms, they must abide by the logical consequences of the stern laws of war. But, as I always believed that we should fight to bring them back into the Union, and should treat them as members of the Union when so brought back, I held that it was a matter of sound policy to do nothing likely to render ultimate reconciliation and harmony impossible, unless such a course were imperative to secure military success.

As the months passed, various circumstances would arise to strain and even damage the relationship that existed between Mac and President Lincoln. Despite the fact that George McClellan's loyalty to the President and particularly to his administration eventually disappeared, there never was a moment when his loyalty to the Constitution or Union faltered.

Even McClellan's critics were forced to acknowledge that he was a superb organizer who knew how to win the admiration and affection of his fighting men. By the end of August, General McClellan had managed to organize and train an army of 75,000 men. These troops were garrisoned on both sides of the Potomac and were everywhere present throughout the city itself. Visitors to Washington could scarcely tell where military camps ended and the civilian or governmental facilities began. Horses, tents, and artillery pieces were carefully stationed throughout the city, which was now very strongly fortified. Foreign diplomats and members of Congress were frequent visitors at the various camps or "tent cities" that circled the capital city.

McClellan was justifiably proud of the amazing improvement he saw as he rode around Washington on his famous black charger named Dan Webster. He was also amused to hear his men wave and cheer loudly as he passed by on his frequent inspection tours. During the training drills that McClellan witnessed, soldiers would often sing a popular song that included the verse, "McClellan's our leader, he's gallant and strong; for God and our country we're marching along!" In slightly over one month, General McClellan had been instrumental in transforming a shattered demoralized mob of soldiers into a grand army. Not bad for a thirty-four year old soldier who had only been a general for several weeks!

In spite of his busy schedule, which included a series of spectacular military parades and reviews, Mac still found time to write his widowed mother who lived in Philadelphia. He wrote stating:

To Elizabeth B. McClellan

My dearest Mother,　　　　　　　*Washington DC Aug. 16, 1861*

I enclose some photographs of your wandering son which the artist insisted upon taking by main force & violence. Please give one to Maria, one to Mary, keep one & give the others to Annie Phillips & the "Coxe girls" with my love. I have a weary time here in exile—a load of cares & anxiety on my mind sufficient to crush any one—difficulties to contend against that you cannot imagine. "The Young General" has no bed of roses on which to recline. I try to do my best & trust in God to assist me for I feel full well that I can do nothing in this great crisis without His aid.

With my truest love to all, ever your affectionate son,

Geo. B. McClellan

As the fall of 1861 began to unfold, various voices from the political and civilian sector began to pressure Congress and the White

House in an effort to get McClellan to launch an offensive against Richmond. The newspapers began to fan the flames of public sentiment, insisting that Mac take his grand army and gain revenge for the slaughter at Bull Run. In many respects, George McClellan had done the job of reorganizing and equipping the Army of the Potomac too quickly and too well. To the untrained politician and zealous abolitionist, McClellan's grand army had overstayed it welcome and must move with speed to justify their existence. Senator Zachariah Chandler summed up the feelings of many in Washington as he publicly stated: "I am greatly dissatisfied with General McClellan. He seems to be devoting himself to parades and military shows instead of cleaning the country of rebels."

In the face of growing criticism, Mac merely kept on with the vital task of fortifying the defense of Washington while directing a handful of skirmishes with tiny Confederate outposts along the Potomac. General McClellan refused to be forced into a major action before his men were ready, and he shared this view with many in Washington. On a private level, Mac told Lincoln that he wanted to accomplish two main things before embarking on a large offensive against the South. First, he wanted to build an army that was large enough to crush the Confederates around Richmond in one major battle, thereby ending the war in dramatic fashion. Also, he wanted to obtain command of the entire Union army, so he would be free to plan and execute the enormous offensive that he envisioned.

At this point in time, Lincoln and many in Washington did not much care where McClellan attacked as long as he attacked quickly and decisively. Virtually all politicians in the North were hungry for some military victory to help boost civilian and military morale. They also needed some significant victory to help maintain the flow of money from financial institutions for the war effort and to secure the ongoing support of foreign powers. For these reasons and others, the White House continued to press General McClellan regarding his military plans. These impatient politicians forgot how they employed these same actions three months earlier against General

Irvin McDowell as he was pushed into committing his green troops into battle prematurely. The result was the disastrous Battle of First Manassas or Bull Run. General George McClellan was not about to allow himself and his men to be forced into fighting the wrong battle at the wrong time just to pacify the politicians in Washington. He would press ahead "with all possible speed."

Very little escaped the attention of the General who commanded the Army of the Potomac. George McClellan understood that his soldiers would only be able to muster the courage they needed for future victory if they drank from the spiritual water that flows from the fountain of Christian faith. As a consequence, General McClellan issued General Order number 7 to his troops on Sept. 6, 1861. The order read as follows:

To General Officers, Army of the Potomac

Head Quarters, Army of the Potomac

General Orders No [7] Washington, Sept. 6, 1861

The Major Gen'l Comd'g desires & requests that in future there may be a more perfect respect for the Sabbath on the part of his command. We are fighting in a holy cause, & should endeavor to deserve the benign favor of the Creator. Unless in the case of an attack by the enemy, or some other extreme military necessity, it is commended to Comd'g officers that all work shall be suspended on the Sabbath, that no unnecessary movements shall be made on that day, that the men shall as far as possible be permitted to rest from their labors, that they shall attend divine service after the customary Sunday morning inspection, & that officers & men shall alike use their influence to ensure the utmost decorum & quiet on that day. The Gen'l Comd'g regards this as no idle form—only a day's rest in seven is necessary to men & animals;—more than this—we owe at least this small tribute of respect to the God of Mercy & of Battles whom we believe to be on our side!

Geo. B. McClellan

Maj. Gen'l Comd'g

Perhaps the greatest significance of the preceding field order, was that it clearly reveals the interest that General McClellan had to live out his Christian faith to a fuller extent than ever before. Prior to his marriage, Mac was only too content to restrict the implications of the Lordship of Christ to the four walls of a church building. Now, however, he was a changed man. He would no longer try to wage war in his own strength, but would correctly view himself as merely an instrument in God's sovereign hands.

The first significant military operation against the Confederates by the Army of the Potomac began in the middle of October. The primary purpose of McClellan was to drive the scattered pockets of Southern troops away from the upper Potomac region. The first big goal in this modest campaign was to occupy the town of Draines-ville, Virginia, before proceeding on to capture the Confederate garrison at Leesburg. McClellan rode out with George McCall's division on October 18, en route to Drainesville on the Virginia side of the Potomac. He wrote his wife, Ellen, on October 19 stating, "I hope to make them abandon Leesburg tomorrow."

The next day, however, proved to be yet another disappointment for the Union cause. As McClellan's contingent of men worked along the Virginia side of the Potomac on their way to Leesburg, another unit under the command of General Stone was riding toward the same objective on the Maryland side of the river. A brief order was sent by McClellan to General Stone directing him to send a small force across the river towards Drainesville, to see if the Confederates would resist or flee. A few hours later, in the face of growing resistance, McClellan decided to order George McCall to return his division to the Washington line. General Stone, who was miles away with his unit, assumed that McCall's men were still pressing on toward Leesburg. As a consequence, he sent a small force across the Potomac for reconnaissance purposes, while directing his brigade commanders to stay put until further notice.

None of the brigade commanders under General Stone realized that he now had the only Union contingent on the Virginia side of the Potomac. This fact resulted in a grave error by volunteer brigade commander Edward D. Baker, as he ordered his brigade to cross over the Potomac on October 21. The Confederate forces in this region were now in an excellent position to concentrate their attack on this small body of Union troops who were pinned against the river. A sharp battle quickly ensued at a location called Ball's Bluff as the men in blue tried desperately to retreat in good order. In the ensuing carnage and confusion, Colonel Baker, who was also a U.S. Senator, was killed. His men were forced to flee into the fast running river where many of them drowned or were shot. Over one thousand Union soldiers lost their lives in this small-scale disaster at Ball's Bluff.

George McClellan referred to this engagement as a "butchery." He sent a memorandum to his commanders, assuring them that the party responsible for the debacle was none other than the inexperienced civilian soldier Edward Baker. He also wrote his wife explaining that the battle was "entirely unauthorized by me and I am in no way responsible for it." Not withstanding the truth of Mac's assessment, the military operation at Ball's Bluff was a rather ugly affair that merely increased the frustration of politicians throughout the North.

In the aftermath of this fresh disappointment, a new round of quarrels erupted between Generals Scott and McClellan. As a result of these well-publicized arguments, Lincoln finally agreed to permit Winfield Scott to retire effective November 1, 1861. During late October, George McClellan received official notification of his advancement to the highest military post in the land. The young Napoleon was now officially general of all the Union armies. He was quick to thank President Lincoln for the appointment, and for taking "several tons off of my shoulders." Abraham Lincoln, in turn, was quick to express to his new general-in-chief the concern he had in regard to overburdening Mac with so heavy a weight of responsibility. He went on to encourage McClellan to "draw on me for all the sense I have, and all the information. In addition to your present command, the supreme command of the army will entail a vast labor upon you." In response to these heartfelt concerns, General McClellan is reported to have said quietly, "I can do it all."

The closing chapter in the military career of Winfield Scott is worth noting. This patriotic warrior had served his country faithfully and well for over fifty years. He fought in the War of 1812 and was at the head of the United States military for decades. His leadership during the Mexican War was invaluable and opened up the possibilities for the expansion of the U.S. in the South and West. By the time of the War Between the States, however, the career of this grand old soldier was in genuine decline. To his credit, Scott had the good sense to acknowledge that he no longer possessed the physical and mental powers necessary to lead the Union army to victory. He therefore packed his trunk on November 2, 1861, and took the next train bound for New York and retirement.

His successor, George McClellan, and several aides went to the train station on the rainy morning of November 3 to say good-by to this feeble old soldier. Scott was visibly moved by McClellan's thoughtfulness, and politely wished Mac every success. "Carry out your own ideas, and you will conquer.... God bless you," said the gracious patriot to his young successor. Winfield Scott also sent his regards to Mac's wife and new little baby girl named May who was born on October 12. Later that day, General McClellan wrote his wife to explain the touching scene that confronted him during Scott's departure.

To Mary Ellen McClellan

[Washington] Nov. 3 [Nov. 2, 1861]

I have already been up this morning—that was at 4 o'clock to escort Gen'l Scott to the depot—it was pitch dark & pouring rain—but with most of the staff & a squadron of cavalry I saw the old man off. He was very polite to me—sent various kind messages to you & the baby—so we parted. The old man said that his sensations were very peculiar in leaving Washn & active life—I can easily understand them—& it may be that at some distant day I too shall totter away from Washn—a worn out soldier, with naught to do but make my peace with God. The sight of this morning was a lesson to me which I hope not soon to forget. I saw there the end of a long, active & ambitious life—the end of the career of the first soldier of his nation—& it was a feeble old man scarce able to walk—hardly any one there to see him off but his successor. Should I ever become vainglorious & ambitious remind me of that spectacle. I pray every night & every morning that I may become neither vain nor ambitious—that I may keep one single object in view, the good of my country. At last I am the "Maj. Gen'l Comd'g the Army"—I do not feel in the least elated, for I do feel the responsibility of the position—& I feel the need for some support. I trust God will aid me....

The very week that McClellan was elevated to supreme commander, he began to receive additional pressure from the White House and Congress to attack the enemy. Mac, meanwhile, continued to plead with President Lincoln. He urged the President "Don't let them hurry me, is all I ask." The response came back from Lincoln time and again, "You shall have your own way in the matter, I assure you, You must not fight until you are ready."

Notwithstanding the sincerity of Lincoln's promises, he simply could not stand by and let the political heat burn him up. He began, therefore, to pursue his new commanding general with relentless fervor. The President simply had to find out when the army would advance. October and November of 1861 were particularly sunny and dry—perfect for a major offensive toward Richmond. This fact only made it more difficult for the President to explain his commander's reluctance to attack. In desperation, Lincoln scheduled a meeting with McClellan at his office to which he also invited Ohio Governor William Dennison and another general. Much to the surprise of Lincoln and his two guests, General McClellan did not show up. The two prominent guests were deeply offended at Mac's unexcused absence while the hapless President simply stated, "Never mind; I will hold McClellan's horse if he will only bring us success."

The President, on one occasion in mid-November attempted an unscheduled visit to General McClellan at his quarters in Washington along with Secretary of State Seward and influential politician,

John Hay. The three visitors arrived at McClellan's quarters only to find that he had not yet returned from a wedding he had decided to attend. One hour later, the weary McClellan returned to his sleeping quarters and was informed by his aid that the President and two men were wanting to see him. Annoyed and reportedly feeling poor, McClellan went directly upstairs and fell right to sleep. Several minutes later, an aid of McClellan politely informed the visitors that the general had gone to bed for the evening. Although the President did not reveal any anger publicly, it was the last time that he would go out of his way to visit George McClellan.

These reported snubbings of Abraham Lincoln by McClellan seem almost hard to comprehend or believe. After all, to readers in the twentieth century, President Lincoln is commonly regarded as a giant of a man and perhaps the greatest leader the United States ever had. How in the world, could a little man like George McClellan fail to stand in awe of the legendary Abe Lincoln? The answer to this question is actually quite simple. The Lincoln of late 1861 was not yet the Lincoln we read of in the history books. At this early stage in his presidency, honest Abe was little more than a struggling Illinois lawyer who turned President by the skin of his teeth. He was not yet legend and was in many respects not particularly impressive. At this point in his career, he was still rather awkward and indecisive. In actual fact, Lincoln had failed to develop a truly comprehensive strategy for the nation in terms of an overarching policy for the war and its aftermath. Consequently, Lincoln would often be pulled and pushed by various radical forces in and out of Congress who did have a definite agenda in view. For these reasons and others, George McClellan did not stand in awe of, nor was he intimidated by the man from Illinois who then occupied the White House. In the final analysis, McClellan gave President Lincoln respect for being honest and well-meaning, but he did not credit Lincoln with any true wisdom in military matters.

Whatever lack of esteem McClellan may have had for Abraham Lincoln, he had even less respect for most of the members of the President's cabinet. Mac had been trained during his West Point days to distrust politicians. Although he was clever enough to work his way through many aspects of the bureaucratic jungle in Washington, he detested the efforts that he was forced to make on behalf of his army. One major mistake that McClellan made in this regard was that he insisted on doing almost all of the administrative groundwork himself. He refused to delegate tasks because he was convinced that his personal touch was needed to ensure that his plans would fall exactly into place. As a result of this mind-set, General McClellan slowly drove himself to the point where he viewed every obstacle in his path as a personal affront. The letters that Mac sent to his wife regarding his growing frustration with personalities in the Lincoln administration clearly reveal that he had begun to view the politicians in Washington as "the enemy in my rear." As we will later see, Mac's unwillingness to play the political game eventually cost him his military career.

"MASTERLY INACTIVITY," OR SIX MONTHS ON THE POTOMAC.

A Northern cartoon mocks Generals McClellan in Washington and Beauregard in Virginia for their inactivity.

The Union armies around Washington, which now numbered 150,000, did not move against the Confederate positions in Virginia during November 1861. One of the main reasons for the inactivity was due to the erroneous intelligence that was accepted by General McClellan and virtually everyone in Washington placing the Confederate troop strength at between 150 and 200 thousand. Only a handful of soldiers or politicians would have the courage to publicly challenge the inflated estimates of the size of the Southern army in Virginia. McClellan would have given a king's ransom to know that the Confederate forces facing him were barely half the size of his own. In the shadow of this false intelligence, General McClellan wrote his wife confessing,

> I cannot move without more means,... and I do not possess the power to control these means.... I am doing all I can to get ready to move before winter sets in, but it now begins to look as if we are condemned to a winter of inactivity.... I have one great comfort in all this—that is I did not seek this position.

The overburdened and ill-informed general-in-chief would soon be confronted with a new wave of problems that stemmed largely from the inactivity of his army. As the weather turned from warm and dry to cold and wet, reports began to surface regarding growing sickness in the tent cities. Army chaplains would almost daily be performing funeral services for young soldiers who succumbed to "camp fever." As the winter began to set in, George McClellan would now need to provide winter quarters and supplies for his men, all 150,000 of them.

By the beginning of December, President Lincoln began to be more assertive in his relationship with the young Napoleon. Like McClellan, the President was sick and tired of holding the hands of fidgety politicians and fiery abolitionists. He therefore proposed that his young general move against Joe Johnston and the Confederates at Manassas Junction immediately and added, "I have a notion to go out with you and stand or fall with the battle." Needless to say, McClellan did not take the President up on his offer.

On December 10, Mac finally responded to the President formally explaining why a direct attack upon the Confederate forces at Manassas Junction would be unprofitable and bloody. He assured Lincoln that he had an alternate plan almost completed that would not be "at all anticipated by the enemy...." The general-in-chief hinted in basic terms about a grand maneuver by way of the Chesapeake Bay that would permit his army to strike at Richmond from the east. This objective, he explained, would force General Johnston to divide his forces around Richmond, and fight the Union army on two fronts. The initial reaction by the President was cautiously hopeful. At least he was able to get some kind of information from his top commander. Still, in Lincoln's situation, he could not help but wonder why Mac's plan needed to be so complicated and costly.

During this time in December, General McClellan was able to travel by train to Baltimore to see his wife and new baby daughter. Two days later, the general returned to his rented home in Washington with his small family in tow. Mrs. Ellen McClellan and her baby were a big hit within social circles in Washington. General McClellan was delighted to see how excellent a hostess his wife had become. She often found time to entertain the many visitors who graced their home at H Street and 15th Avenue.

By the end of 1861, the patience of the radical members of Congress had formally come to an end. These influential politicians were no longer going to wait for answers from the White House or the military command. In mid-December, a Joint Committee on the Conduct of War was established in Congress, headed by Republican radical Benjamin Wade from Ohio. The purpose of the Committee was to establish who was responsible for the inactivity of the army, and to whatever extent possible, crucify all offenders. Shortly before Christmas, the Committee scheduled a hearing and invited George McClellan to be its first witness. Mac agreed to testify on December 23, but was unable to attend this meeting due to illness. As it turned out, McClellan and his chief of staff, Randolph Marcy had contracted typhoid fever and would be confined to bed for weeks. Rumors began to fly to the effect that the general-in-chief was close

Mr. and Mrs. George B. McClellan

to death. Other rumors, spread by extremists in Congress who hated McClellan, indicated that Mac was merely using the garb of illness to escape Congressional accountability.

The real truth was that Mac was a very sick man, but never in genuine danger of dying. Lincoln tried to reassure all factions in Congress that McClellan would soon have the army in the field, but they insisted on having the general himself explain why he had only been able to make the politicians in Washington perfectly safe from attack. The political posturing of President Lincoln was totally ineffectual. As usual, Lincoln wanted to try to please all sides. The end result of this strategy was that the President never moved fast enough for the radical members of Congress and yet rarely moved slow enough for those politicians that were paranoid about a Confederate attack on Washington. The President, fully aware of his failure before Congress sent a letter to Mac urging him to appear before the committee as soon as his health would allow.

The year 1862 finally arrived and almost everyone in the North was happy to see the old year end. By most any measure, the year 1861 had been a bad year for the Union cause. The future of the soldier from Philadelphia, George McClellan, was also grey and foreboding as he opened the new year on a bed of illness and political controversy. He would not stay in bed very long, however, for word came to him from a political acquaintance named Edwin Stanton that Lincoln had scheduled a special meeting of his generals and various cabinet members for January 13 to talk about the future of the Army of the Potomac.

On the day before Lincoln's special meeting, General McClellan managed to gather enough strength to stop by and visit the President at the White House. During their discussions, Lincoln made it clear that he was finished with the waiting game and that he would like to "borrow" McClellan's army if he in fact had no immediate plans to use it. This dialogue prompted the young general to reveal to the President a clearer and more detailed explanation of his battle plan. Lincoln listened with interest as Mac described the research and planning that his staff had already put into the campaign to float 120,000 troops down the Chesapeake Bay to Fort Monroe for a speedy attack on Richmond.

The next afternoon, January 13, the President met with McClellan, various members of his cabinet, and generals McDowell, Franklin, and Meigs. Lincoln opened the meeting by briefly stating his purposes for the gathering and then requested commentary from the assembled generals on future military options. Generals McDowell and Franklin began to comment on the pro's and con's of a direct land based attack against Richmond from the North versus a turning movement against Richmond by way of the Chesapeake Bay. When it came time for Mac to speak he simply stated, "You are entitled to have any opinion you please!" It was very clear to everyone present that George McClellan was deeply disturbed by the entire spectacle. He made very few comments during the meeting and toward the end of the gathering stated,

> I will not reveal my plans unless ordered to do so by the President.
> No general fit to command an army will ever submit his plans to
> the judgment of such an assembly.... If I tell my plans, they will be
> in the *New York Herald* tomorrow morning....

Secretary of War, Edwin Stanton

The President's meeting was not a comfortable one, but at least General McClellan was out of bed and talkative. Later on the thirteenth, Mac learned that Lincoln had appointed his old political ally Edwin Stanton as the Secretary of War in place of the resigning Simon Cameron. Several hours later, Stanton appeared at Mac's home under the guise of soliciting his support for the upcoming confirmation hearings in the Senate. Edwin Stanton had served as Attorney General under the Buchanan Administration and was a consummate Washington bureaucrat in the worst sense of the term. He was power-hungry, unprincipled, sneaky, and a compulsive liar who was not opposed to using a political office for personal gain. Unhappily for George McClellan, he would only discover the true character of Stanton after he had been abused by this ungodly schemer.

The memoirs of General McClellan include a brief description of his relationship with Edwin Stanton, both before and after his appointment as Secretary of War. Mac states:

> I had never seen Mr. Stanton... before reaching Washington in 1861. Not many weeks after arriving I was introduced to him as a safe adviser on legal points. From that moment he did his best to ingratiate himself with me, and professed the warmest friendship and devotion. I had no reason to suspect his sincerity, and therefore believed him to be what he professed. The most disagreeable thing about him was the extreme virulence with which he abused the President, the Administration, and the Republican Party. He carried this to such an extent that I was often shocked by it. He never spoke of the President in any other way than as the 'original gorilla.'...
>
> At some time during the autumn of 1861 Secretary Cameron made quite an abolition speech to some newly arrived regiment. Next day Stanton urged me to arrest him for inciting to insubordination. He often advocated the propriety of my seizing the government and taking affairs into my own hands. As he always expressed himself in favor of putting down the rebellion at any cost, I always regarded these extreme views as the ebullitions of an intense and patriotic nature, and sometimes wasted more or less time in endeavoring to bring him to more moderate views, never dreaming that all the while this man was in close communication with the very men whom he so violently abused....
>
> Finally, one day when I returned to my house from my day's work and was dressing for dinner... Mr. Stanton's card came up, and as

soon as possible I went down to see him. He told me that he had been appointed Secretary of War and that his name had been sent to the Senate for confirmation, and that he had called to confer with me as to his acceptance. He said that acceptance would involve very great personal sacrifices on his part, and that the only possible inducement would be that he might have it in his power to aid me in the work of putting down the rebellion; that he was willing to devote all his time, intellect, and energy to my assistance, and that together we could soon bring the war to an end. If I wished him to accept he would do so, but only on my account; that he had come to know my wishes and would determine accordingly. I told him that I hoped he would accept the position.

Stanton thus made certain that McClellan would not oppose his confirmation. McClellan goes on:

Soon after Mr. Stanton became Secretary of War it became clear that without any reason known to me, our relations had completely changed. Instead of using his new position to assist me he threw every obstacle in my way, and did all in his power to create difficulty and distrust between the President and myself. I soon found it impossible to gain access to him. Before he was in office he constantly ran after me and professed the most ardent friendship; as soon as he became Secretary of War his whole manner changed, and I could no longer find the opportunity to transact even the ordinary current business of the office with him.

On January 15, George McClellan testified at the Congressional Committee regarding the status of the Army of the Potomac and his knowledge of the military operations at Ball's Bluff. The hearing was relatively uneventful as the controversial general gave the audience a vague promise that his army would spring into action soon. The committee permitted Mac to side step the issue of Ball's Bluff and threw the weight of their criticism against Brigadier General Charles P. Stone. This Union officer was eventually arrested under suspicion of collaboration with the enemy, but was later released without ever being charged with a crime. McClellan's assessment of the Stone affair was that the members of the committee were hungry for a scapegoat. "They want a victim," was the honest reaction of General McClellan.

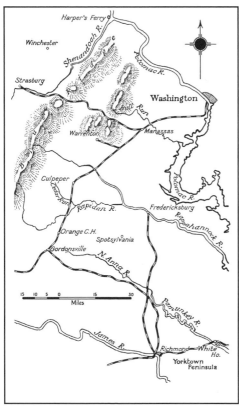

Map of Eastern Virginia

While the worthless Congressional hearings were winding down, President Lincoln was gearing up for a showdown with McClellan. He issued General Order Number 1 in late January demanding an offensive movement of all Union land and naval forces by February 22, 1862. This directive from the commander-in-chief apparently prompted Mac to lay out his full plan before Lincoln for a movement by sea to the Peninsula east of Richmond. As already explained, President Lincoln had heard some of the plans of General McClellan for an offensive down the Chesapeake Bay in early December. The President now knew the full details of this plan but he was still clinging to his original reservations. He asked McClellan why a more straightforward land based attack along the Occoguan River line would not be less risky and less costly than a grand amphibious assault. McClellan was not eager to debate military strategy with a novice but, nevertheless, he decided to supply the President with a detailed report in defense of his Peninsula strategy.

Abraham Lincoln received the twenty-two page report from his general-in-chief on February 3 and discussed it's merits and demerits with Secretary of War Stanton and others. At this same time, good news came in from the West as a late winter offensive by General Grant's troops successfully captured two Confederate forts in Kentucky. Suddenly, the center of the Confederate defensive line was cracked and Tennessee now laid open to attack. Several days later, more good news reached Washington as Union General Buell occupied Nashville on February 25.

While McClellan waited for Lincoln to give his approval for the operation he recommended, he initiated a small but strategic movement to Harper's Ferry. It was the general's intention to rebuild the important railroad lines and bridge at Harper's Ferry so that Union forces could move more quickly and efficiently into the Shenandoah Valley region. As usual, this operation had its share of problems, but eventually the goals of this mission were accomplished.

General Ulysses S. Grant

On March 8, McClellan was ordered to meet with President Lincoln at the White House. The general-in-chief assumed that the President was interested in trying to finalize a battle strategy against Richmond during this meeting, however, this was not the case. Lincoln told Mac that he was not satisfied with the way things were handled at Harper's Ferry and that he was even more concerned with an "ugly" report that had surfaced concerning the general's future intentions. The President went on to say that he had been told that the real motive for McClellan's "traitorous" plan was to take his army away from Washington in order to leave it open to Confederate attack. Immediately after hearing these words, General McClellan jumped to his feet and demanded a retraction of the charge. Although Lincoln went on to explain that he was merely repeating what he was told, Mac asked the President to be more careful in the future before casting any doubt upon his intentions. At the close of this peculiar meeting, General McClellan told Lincoln that he would place his Urbanna or Peninsula plan before his entire staff of twelve generals so the President could objectively decide "whether he was a traitor or not."

Several hours later, Mac met with his generals to brief them on his military strategy and to ask them to cast their vote for or against his plan. The results of this vote were delivered to the White House in person by each of the generals who were thoroughly interrogated by Secretary Stanton. The final vote fell out squarely in favor of McClellan's plan; consequently, Lincoln felt obliged to approve this operation. The only condition that Lincoln placed upon his decision was that the move down the Chesapeake Bay must not unduly weaken the defenses at Washington. This condition did not disturb General McClellan, for he had already pledged to the President that the capital city would remain safe while he attacked Richmond.

The following day, President Lincoln prepared two additional war orders. His first directive established a new command structure for the Army of the Potomac. The second order repeated the priority of protecting the city of Washington and directed the opening troop movements down the Chesapeake to begin no later than March 18. Although the young Napoleon was annoyed at the "meddling" of the President in regard to military matters, in actual fact almost none of these war orders were disturbing to McClellan. Only later would Mac come to view the commanders that Lincoln appointed as part of a political scheme "to secure the failure of the coming campaign."

As the Army of the Potomac was readying itself to take the field, an alarming report was received in Washington on March 9. This report stated that the Confederate ironclad *Merrimack* (also known

A photograph of McClellan and members of his staff show the Prince de Joinville (*second from right*) and his nephew, the Comte de Paris (*far right*), who served as an aide-de-camp.

as the *Virginia*) steamed out into the waters of the Chesapeake Bay and destroyed two of the navy's wooden frigates at Hampton Roads and drove a third ship aground. McClellan and various notables were summoned to the White House for a military counsel. Clearly, the Union leaders had a crisis on their hands. While the military leaders talked and schemed, new information arrived that brought a quick end to the crisis. The Union ironclad *Monitor* had steamed over to Hampton Roads and fought the *Merrimack* to a draw and forced her to return to the safety of the port of Norfolk. This brief engagement changed the face of naval warfare forever. Almost overnight, wooden war ships became destined for the scrap heap.

For George McClellan, the most significant aspect of this historic naval battle was that it forced him to change his destination from the port city of Urbanna to Ft. Monroe, farther down the Peninsula. Since his original plans already contained a provision to send troops to Fort Monroe if "worse come to worse," this strange turn of events merely required the young general to slightly modify his plans.

On March 12, General McClellan read a newspaper article that informed him of the fact that he had been removed from the post of general-in-chief and that he was demoted to the level of Major General of the Army of the Potomac. The newspaper went on to indicate that Lincoln's latest war order also appointed General Halleck to command the Union armies in the west, while leaving the position of general-in-chief vacant "until otherwise ordered." This presidential order in effect put Lincoln and Stanton in the position of running the war themselves. A situation which Edwin Stanton would take full advantage of at the expense of George McClellan.

General McClellan was eventually briefed by the former governor of Ohio, William Dennison, regarding the actual intentions of Lincoln in regard to his most recent order. Mac was reassured that the President still had every confidence in his ability to command and that the changes were made in an effort to free him from conflicts and pressures that he did not need. After this explanation, McClellan did not continue to harbor ill feelings toward President Lincoln. He, in fact, put the confusing and depressing situation in the best light possible, as he thought about how nice it will be to simply concentrate on leading the Army of the Potomac to victory. McClellan also discussed these events with his chief of staff, Randolph Marcy, and said, "I think the less I see of Washington the better." For good reason, General McClellan welcomed the opportunity to take the field and face some new enemies for a change.

Part of the reason for the gloom and distemper that was emanating from the White House was that Abraham and Mary Todd Lincoln had a great personal tragedy befall them in February. The eleven year old son of Mr. and Mrs. Lincoln, named Willie, died after a brief illness. This boy was President Lincoln's pride and joy, and the loss was a crushing blow to this statesman and father. During the period of official mourning, General McClellan, who himself had recently become a father, wrote a tender letter of condolence to his sorrowful chief. Mac stated in part that he grieved with the President on account of "the sad calamity that has befallen you and your family. You have been a kind and true friend to me in the midst of the great cares and difficulties by which we have been surrounded during the past few months—your confidence has upheld me when

I should otherwise have felt weak. I wish now only to assure you and your family that I have felt the deepest sympathy in your affliction." As General McClellan prepared to leave Washington in March, President Lincoln would be one of his few remaining friends at the capital.

The confusion and general tension that was so evident in the city of Washington at this time stood in noticeable contrast to the city of Richmond. The Confederate States picked the happy occasion of the birth of a famous Virginian, George Washington, to inaugurate their first President. On February 22, 1862, President Jefferson Davis stood on a platform in the center of Richmond and took the oath of office amidst a crowd of supporters. As raindrops danced among the crowds of people, a lady by the name of Sallie Putnam, who was present at the inauguration, recorded these observations.

> A covered platform had been erected just underneath, or beside the Washington Monument, where the brazen image of "the Father of his Country" looked down upon this singular sight in the capital of his native state, seeming to watch with interest the novel proceedings—with his arm outstretched to shield the platform beneath, and his finger pointed southward. It seemed to us, of the hopeful class, significant.

> Very few heard the inaugural address. The pattering of the rain on the carriages and the umbrellas… prevented the sound of the human voice from reaching our ears.

> A newsman who was near Davis noted that the address was "characterized by great dignity, united with much feeling and grace, especially the closing sentence. Throwing up his eyes and hands to heaven he said, 'With humble gratitude and adoration, acknowledging the Providence which has so visibly protected the Confederacy during its brief but eventful career, to Thee, O God, I trustingly commit myself, and prayerfully invoke Thy blessing on my country and its cause.'"

This lady of the South also pointed out the nearly universal support that Jefferson Davis enjoyed as he entered his new public office.

Mrs. Putnam stated, "Never was there a man put into power so nearly by public acclamation as Mr. Davis.... No other was mentioned as his competitor for office."

The city of Richmond was about to lose its peaceful tranquillity, however, as General McClellan issued orders to begin his campaign that would eventually hurl over 120,000 men directly at the Confederate forces stationed there.

The first wave of troops moved to the embarkation point at Alexandria, a few miles from the capital and read the long awaited directive from their chieftain. McClellan wrote:

To the Army of the Potomac

Soldiers of the Army

Headquarters: Army of the Potomac!

Fairfax Court House, Va., March 14, 1862

For a long time I have kept you inactive, but not without a purpose: you were to be disciplined, armed and instructed; the formidable artillery you now have, had to be created; other armies were to move and accomplish certain results. I have held you back that you might give the deathblow to the rebellion that has distracted our once happy country. The patience you have shown, and your confidence in your General, are worth a dozen victories. These preliminary results are now accomplished. I feel that the patient labors of many months have produced their fruit; the Army of the Potomac is now a real Army,—magnificent in material, admirable in discipline and instruction, excellently equipped and armed;—your commanders are all that I could wish. The moment for action has arrived, and I know that I can trust in you to save our country. As I ride through your ranks, I see in your faces the sure presage of victory; I feel that you will do whatever I ask of you. The period of inaction has passed. I will bring you now face to face with the rebels, and only pray that God may defend the right. In whatever direction you may move, however strange my actions may appear to you, ever bear in mind that my [destiny] is linked with yours, and that all I do is to bring you, where I know you wish to be,—on the decisive battlefield. It is my business to place you there. I am to watch over you as a parent over his children; and you know that your General loves you from the depths of his heart. It shall be my care, as it has ever been, to gain success with the least possible loss; but I know that, if it is necessary, you will willingly follow me to our graves, for our righteous cause. God smiles upon us, victory attends us, yet I would not have you think that our aim is to be attained without a manly struggle. I will not disguise it from you: you have brave foes to encounter, foemen well worthy of the steel that you will use so well. I shall demand of you great, heroic exertions, rapid and long marches, desperate combats, privations, perhaps. We will share all these together; and when this sad war is over we will all return to our homes, and feel that we can ask no higher honor than the proud consciousness that we belonged to the Army of the Potomac.

Geo. B. McClellan

Major General Commanding

McClellan's amazing armada began its historic voyage down the Chesapeake on March 17, 1862. Ships of every size, over 400 in all, took part in the amphibious operation that an English observer called "the stride of a giant." It would take days for the men, horses, military ordinance, and equipment to be shuttled to their destination at Fort Monroe. As for General McClellan, he climbed aboard the steamer *Commodore* bound for the Peninsula and Fort Monroe.

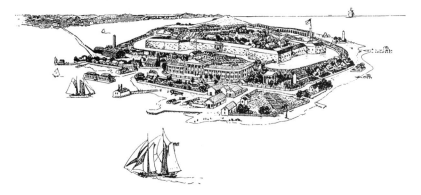

Fort Monroe and the Old Hygeia Hotel

Chapter Eight

General McClellan and the Grand Army

SUMMER 1862

The thousands of soldiers who sailed down the Chesapeake in late March 1862, had quite an exhilarating experience. The mere size of the operation was enough to impress almost anyone. Each soldier, in his own way, would remember this amazing voyage. They each knew that they were making history.

Many interesting accounts of this voyage were recorded by the men who took part in the historic Peninsular Campaign. An army chaplain by the name of Stewart wrote the following comments regarding some of his experiences during the journey:

> Neither the novelties of our condition, the tumult of the voyage, nor the dense throng of the boat, were permitted to interfere with or interrupt our accustomed evening worship.... A goodly number got together, on the fore and upper deck of the boat, and united in songs of praise, in prayer, and in words of exhortation and encouragement. The position, the scenery, and the uncertainties of our journey all combined to render our evening worship peculiarly interesting and profitable.

> At night we were on the broad Chesapeake. A stiff breeze set our fleet rocking, but we slept quietly, leaving the waves to take care of themselves and the pilots to take care of the boats.

Again in the words of Chaplain Stewart:

> Waking at dawn... we found our old New York and Fall River boat safely anchored directly in front of Fortress Monroe.... The fortifications are situated on a low point of sandy beach.... By good engineering, enormous expense, and labor long-continued, the fort

has been rendered one of the strongest in the world.... It is almost the only fortified place in all Dixie saved to the Union. Here stretches, far away towards the ocean, the beautiful Chesapeake; there the bay-like mouth of the James; yonder the misty view of Norfolk and Portsmouth; around us an immense fleet.

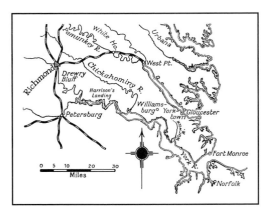

Richmond, Virginia, and Vicinity

A Union army surgeon named Stevens, explains what he witnessed upon reaching Fort Monroe:

Dense masses of infantry, long trains of artillery, and thousands of cavalry, with unnumbered army wagons and mules were mingled in grand confusion along the shore. The neighing of horses, the braying of mules, the rattle of wagons and artillery, and the sound of many voices mingled in one grand inharmonious concert.

Private Warren Goss marveled at the scene's intermixture of colors:

The red cap, white leggings, and baggy trousers of Zouaves mingled with the blue uniforms and dark trimmings of the regular infantrymen, the short jackets and yellow trimmings of the cavalry, the red stripes of the artillery, and the dark blue with orange trimmings of the engineers; together with the ragged, many-colored costumes of the black laborers and teamsters.

As soon as General McClellan was sure that his troops were disembarking and forming up in good order at Fort Monroe, he began a movement upon Yorktown. In light of the fact that Confederate forces had been entrenched in Yorktown since the beginning of the war, Mac assumed that their fortifications were formidable. The

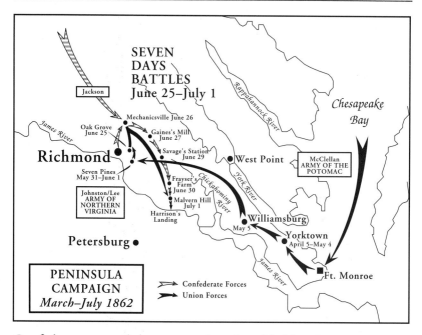

Confederate general that was stationed at this historic town was one of many shrewd officers bent on deceiving McClellan. Major General John B. Magruder was determined to stall the Army of the Potomac in advance of Yorktown.

This general produced a number of artifices and impressive feats to mislead Mac into believing that he must lay siege to Yorktown before advancing up the Peninsula. Counterfeit gun emplacements dotted the hillsides as General Magruder regularly moved his small unit of 15,000 men to different locations along the Confederate line in order to mislead the Union scouts who were busy estimating enemy troop strengths. All of this deception, along with some well placed sharpshooters and artillery positions, enabled the Southern general to convince McClellan that he needed to advance slowly but surely by way of a siege. During this opening engagement, General McClellan made the tactical decision that it was better to move cautiously than risk the needless loss of human life. As usual, Mac made his decisions by the book—that is, the West Point book—which stated that it was unwise to throw men headlong into fixed fortifications.

General McClellan was not the only Union soldier to be intimidated by the fortifications at Yorktown. An interesting account of the battlefield around Yorktown was penned by Union Private Warren Lee Goss. This soldier stated that:

> We pitched our camp on Wormley Creek, near the Moore house, on the York River, in sight of the enemy's water-battery and their defensive works at Gloucester Point. One of the impediments to an immediate attack on Yorktown was the difficulty of using light artillery in the muddy fields in our front, and at that time the topography of the country ahead was but little understood and had to be learned by reconnaissance in force. We had settled down to the siege of Yorktown; began bridging the streams between us and the enemy, constructing and improving the roads for the rapid transit of supplies, and for the advance. The first parallel was opened about a mile from the enemy's fortifications, extending

A so-called "Quaker Gun"—a log carved, mounted, and painted black to resembled a cannon—guards an abandoned Confederate fortification.

along the entire front of their works, which reached from the York River on the left to Warwick Creek on the right, along a line about four miles in length. Fourteen batteries and three redoubts were planted, heavily armed with ordinance.

We were near Battery No. 1, not far from the York River. On it were mounted several 200-pounder guns, which commanded the enemy's water-batteries. One day I was in a redoubt on the left, and saw General McClellan with the Prince de Joinville, examining the enemy's works through their field-glasses. They very soon drew the fire

Confederate Sharpshooters Watch the York River

of the observant enemy, who opened with one of their heavy guns on the groups, sending the first shot howling and hissing over and very close to their heads; another, quickly following it, struck in the parapet of the redoubt. The French prince, seemingly quite startled, jumped and glanced nervously around, while McClellan quietly knocked the ashes from his cigar.

Several of our war-vessels made their appearance in the York River, and occasionally threw a shot at the enemy's works; but most of them were kept busy at Hampton Roads, watching for the iron-clad *Merrimack*, which was still afloat. The firing from the enemy's lines was of little consequence, not amounting to over ten or twelve shots each day, a number of these being directed at the huge balloon which went up daily on a tour of inspection, from near General Fitz John Porter's headquarters. One day the balloon broke from its mooring of ropes and sailed majestically over the enemy's works; but fortunately for its occupants it soon met a counter-current of air which returned it safe to our lines. The month of April was a dreary one, much of the time rainy and uncomfortable. It was a common expectation among us that we were about to end the rebellion. One of my comrades wrote home to his father that we should probably finish up the war in season for him to be at home to teach the village school the following winter; in fact, I believe he partly engaged to teach it. Another wrote to his mother: "We have got them hemmed in on every side, and the only reason they don't run is because they can't." We had at last corduroyed every road and bridged every creek; our guns and mortars were in position; Battery No. 1 had actually opened on the enemy's works; Saturday, May 3, 1862, and it was expected that our whole line would open on them in the morning. About 2 o'clock on Saturday night, or rather on Sunday morning, while on guard duty, I observed a bright illumination, as if a fire had broken out within the enemy's lines. Several guns were fired from their works during the early morning hours, but soon after daylight on May 4 it was reported that they had abandoned their works in our front, and we very quickly found the report to be true. As soon as I was relieved from guard duty, I went over on "French leave" to view our enemy's fortifications. They were prodigiously strong. A few tumble-down tents and houses and seventy pieces of heavy ordinance had been abandoned as the price of the enemy's safe retreat.

As soon as it was known that the Confederates had abandoned the works at Yorktown, the commanding general sent the cavalry and horse artillery under Stoneman in pursuit to harass the retreating column. The infantry divisions of Smith (Fourth Corps) and Hooker (Third Corps) were sent forward by two roads to support the light column. General Sumner (the officer second in rank in the Army of the Potomac) was directed to proceed to the front and assume command until McClellan's arrival. Stoneman overtook Johnston's rear-guard about noon, six miles from Williamsburg, and skirmished with the cavalry of J. E. B. Stuart, following sharply until 4 o'clock, when he was confronted by a line of redoubts before Williamsburg.

Confederate Positions Outside Williamsburg

While General McClellan was establishing the siege operation at Yorktown that was just described, he discovered that Lincoln and Stanton were no longer going to send him the 40,000 troops under McDowell as originally promised. Despite the appeals of McClellan for the safety of his army and the success of his operation, Lincoln would not permit McDowell's corps to leave the Shenandoah Valley where the President felt they were needed to discourage Thomas "Stonewall" Jackson from laying siege to Washington. McClellan was therefore reduced to a beggar at a critical time in his operations. He wired the White House pleading, "Do not force me to fight with diminished numbers."

Two days after the Confederate occupants at Yorktown retreated up the Peninsula, the advanced guard of McClellan's forces broke through and occupied Williamsburg on May 6, 1862. The battle at Williamsburg, like Yorktown, was relatively bloodless and Mac was quick to boast of this fact.

This boasting was not appreciated by the leaders at Washington. They wanted an immediate and bold move on Richmond town and not another telegram from McClellan requesting more troops. All of the attempts by Mac to explain his growing problems with inadequate equipment, insufficient reinforcements, and lousy rain-soaked roads were to no avail. To the White House, these problems were essentially more excuses designed to justify inaction.

Siege of Yorktown

Over the many years since the War Between the States, numerous historians have sought to blame George McClellan for having the "slows." They deride Mac for his inability or reluctance to accurately comprehend the true size and strength of the Confederate forces that he faced on the Peninsula. It should be asked, however, is this commonly held opinion, on balance, fair and accurate? No. In the first place, Lincoln and his cabinet members, along with almost all of the top Union generals, accepted the inaccurate intelligence figures concocted by Allen Pinkerton both before and during the Peninsula campaign. General McClellan clearly expressed his opinion that Richmond was protected by 175 to 200 thousand enemy troops and that an additional 60,000 Confederate soldiers were in the Shenandoah Valley. These figures were, indeed, inaccurate but they were the commonly accepted intelligence of that time within virtually all political and military circles in the North. Why is it then that McClellan should be the only personality to be labeled as paranoid? Was it not Lincoln and the top Union generals that individually approved McClellan's Peninsula plans based upon the belief that there were 150-175 thousand Confederates guarding the approaches to Richmond? Furthermore, if Lincoln and his armchair generals were so calm and discerning, then why did they break their promise to McClellan and keep 40,000 extra soldiers to defend Washington from Thomas Jackson's brigade of 9,000 men when the Northern capital was already guarded by over 35,000 troops?

The answers to these questions cut to the real heart of the reasons why there was a lack of proper support for McClellan's plans. The honest fact is that the leaders in Washington had come to the point of distrusting McClellan. Having brought themselves to this view, it was but a small step to begin cutting off support for him. They simply refused to believe that he was willing to prosecute the war in a manner that they thought was desirable. Although it is certainly true that McClellan was, on occasion, overly cautious as a field commander; the real problem that the radicals in Washington had with their young general was his absolute insistence on waging war in a Christian manner. He would not go along with efforts to improperly "appropriate" the private property of Southerners. McClellan also refused to wage war on civilians, prisoners of war, and southern institutions. His Christian principles would not permit him to play fast and loose with the lives of his men. Mac was the type of general who would literally stay up half the night trying to figure out how he could win a battle in a manner that would spare as many lives as possible on both sides of the battlefield. In the final analysis, the insistence of General McClellan to do all things decently and in order drove the unprincipled radicals in Washington berserk. In their madness, they lashed out at one of the few Union generals who truly understood the art of war based on humane and Christian principles.

It should also be understood that the reasons that McClellan gave for his army's slowness to press into Richmond had considerable merit. Mac's troops had to literally build wooden planked roads for the horses and artillery to travel on during their offensive up the Peninsula. Private Warren Lee Goss of the Army of the Potomac painted quite an accurate picture of the true military significance of mud soaked roads to an advancing army as he wrote the following:

> After we passed the fort, which commanded the bridge on the Virginia side, we encountered one of the most powerful allies of the

"The mud was in constant league with the enemy...."

enemy, particularly during the winter and spring campaigns in Virginia,—MUD. No country equals a Virginia road for mud. We struck it thick, and sometimes knee-deep. It was very "heavy marching." The foot sank insidiously into the mud, and came out again reluctantly; it had to be coaxed, and while you were persuading your left, the willing right was sinking as deep. The noise of the walking was like that of a suction-pump when the water is exhausted.

The order was given, "Route step"; we climbed the banks of the road in search of firm earth, but it couldn't be found, so we went on pumping away, making about one foot in depth to two in advance. Our feet seemingly weighed twenty pounds each. We carried a number six into the unknown depths of mud, but it came out a number twelve, elongated, yellow, and nasty. Occasionally a boot or shoe would be left in the mud, and it would take an exploring expedition to find it. Wad River declared that though Virginia was once in the Union, she was now in the mud. The boys called their shoes "pontoons," "mud-hooks," "soil-excavators," and other names not quite so polite.

The mud was in constant league with the enemy; an efficient ally in defensive warfare; equivalent to reinforcements of twenty thousand infantry. To realize the situation, spread tar a foot deep all over your backyard, and then try to walk through it; particularly is this experiment recommended to those citizens who were constantly crying, "Why doesn't the army move?"

Mud took the military valor all out of a man. Any one would think, from reading the Northern newspapers, that we soldiers had macadamized roads over which to charge at the enemy. It would have pleased us much to have seen those "On to Richmond" people put over a 5-mile course in the Virginia mud, loaded with a 40-pound knapsack, 60 rounds of cartridges, and haversacks filled with 4 days' rations.

Without exaggeration, the mud has never had full credit for the immense help it afforded the enemy, as it prevented us from advancing upon them. The ever-present foe, winter and spring, in Old Virginia, was Mud.

In addition to the problems caused by rain, General McClellan had good reasons to suspect that his reinforcements were not going to arrive when he needed them. He wrote a detailed explanation in

Barge Ferrying Artillery, Gunners, and Infantry

his memoirs regarding how he lost control of the means to reinforce his army during the Peninsula campaign.

> While at Fairfax Court House, on the 12th of March, I learned that there had appeared in the daily papers the order relieving me from the general command of all the armies and confining my authority to the Department of the Potomac. I had received no previous intimation of the intention of the Government in this respect. Thus, when I embarked for Fort Monroe on the 1st of April, my command extended from Philadelphia to Richmond, from the Alleghenies, including the Shenandoah, to the Atlantic; for an order had been issued a few days previous placing Fort Monroe and the Department of Virginia under my command, and authorizing me to withdraw from the troops therein ten thousand, to form a division to be added to the First Corps.

> The fortifications of Washington were at this time completed and armed. I had already given instructions for the refortification of Manassas, the reopening of the Manassas Gap Railroad, the protection of its bridges by block-houses, the entrenchment of a position for a brigade at or near the railroad crossing of the Shenandoah, and an entrenched post at Chester Gap. I left about 42,000 troops for the immediate defense of Washington, and more than 35,000 for the Shenandoah Valley—an abundance to insure the safety of Washington and to check any attempt to recover the lower Shenandoah and threaten Maryland. Beyond this force, the reserves of the Northern States were all available.

> On my arrival at Fort Monroe on the 2d of April, I found five divisions of infantry, Sykes's brigade of regulars, two regiments of cavalry, and a portion of the reserve artillery disembarked. Another cavalry regiment and a part of a fourth had arrived, but were still on shipboard; comparatively few wagons had come. On the same day came a telegram stating that the Department of Virginia was withdrawn from my control, and forbidding me to form the division of ten thousand men without General Wool's sanction. I was thus deprived of the command of the base of operations, and the ultimate strength of the army was reduced to 135,000—another

serious departure from the plan of campaign.

Just at this moment came a telegram, dated the 4th, informing me that the First Corps was withdrawn from my command. Thus, when too deeply committed to recede, I found that another reduction of about 43,000, including several cavalry regiments withheld from me, diminished my paper force to 92,000, instead of the 155,000 on which the plans of the campaign had been founded, and with which it was intended to operate. The number of men left behind sick and from other causes incident to such a movement, reduced the total for duty to some 85,000, from which must be deducted all camp, depot, and train guards, escorts, and non-combatants, such as cooks, servants, orderlies, and extra-duty men in the various staff-departments, which reduced the numbers actually available for battle to some 67,000 or 68,000.

The order withdrawing the First Corps also broke up the Department of the Potomac, forming out of it the Department of the Shenandoah, under General Banks, and the Department of the Rappahannock, under General McDowell, the latter including Washington. I thus lost all control of the depots at Washington, as I had already been deprived of the control of the base at Fort Monroe and of the ground subsequently occupied by the depot at White House. The only territory remaining under my command was the paltry triangle between the departments of the Rappahannock and Virginia; even that was yet to be won from the enemy. I was thus relieved from the duty of providing for the safety of Washington, and deprived of all control over the troops in that vicinity. Instead of one directing head controlling operations which should have been inseparable, the region from the Alleghenies to the sea was parceled out among four independent commanders.

On the 3d of April, at the very moment of all other when it was most necessary to push recruiting most vigorously, to make good the inevitable losses in battle and by disease, an order was issued from the War Department discontinuing all recruiting for the volunteers and breaking up all their recruiting stations. Instead of a regular and permanent system of recruiting, whether by voluntary enlistment or by draft, a spasmodic system of large drafts was thereafter resorted to, and, to a great extent, the system of forming new regiments. The results were wasteful and pernicious. There were enough, or nearly enough, organizations in the field, and these should have been constantly maintained at the full strength by a regular and constant influx of recruits, who, by association with their veteran comrades, would soon have become efficient. The new regiments required much time to become useful, and endured very heavy and unnecessary losses from disease and in battle owing to the inexperience of the officers and men. A course more in accordance with the best-established military principles and the uniform experience of war would have saved the country millions of treasure and thousands of valuable lives.

In spite of the uncertain support and a lack of reinforcements, General McClellan would need to press on to the best of his ability. The Army of the Potomac had a job to do, and the young Napoleon would have to make the best of a difficult situation.

After the battle of Williamsburg, General McClellan decided to consolidate his forces that were scattered between Yorktown, Williamsburg, and the mouth of the Pamunkey River. He did not want to give the enemy the opportunity to strike an isolated portion of his invasion force and possibly cut it off from his main army. On the 10th of May, the Army of the Potomac was again united and proceeded to move toward Richmond once again.

This same evening, Mac wrote a series of brief letters to his loved ones back home. These letters summarize McClellan's situation at this particular point. He wrote:

> *To Mary Ellen McClellan*
>
> *May 10 [1862] Saturday 11:45 P.M.*
>
> *Camp 19 miles from Williamsburg*
>
> *...[I] am encamped now at an old wooden church, & in easy communication with Franklin, Porter &c. Fitz came over to see me this afternoon & I go over to see him & Franklin tomorrow. Tomorrow being Sunday I give the men a rest—merely closing up some of the troops in*

Gunboat on the Pamunkey River

rear. I begin to find some Union sentiment in this country....

I expect to fight a very severe battle on the Chickahominy, but feel no doubt as to the result. All my officers & men have unlimited confidence in me—I saw the effect of my presence the other day in front of Wmsburg—& the men all felt the change—they behaved superbly & will do better if possible next time. Tomorrow I will get up supplies—reorganize—arrange details & get ready for the great fight—feeling that I shall lose nothing by respecting Sunday as far as I can. Secesh[2] is gathering all he can in front of me—so much the better—I will finish the matter by one desperate blow. I have implicit confidence in my men & they in me! What more can I ask....

Sunday [May 11] 8 A.M. As I told you last night I am giving my men some rest today—they need it much—for they have for some time been living on long marches, short rations & rainy bivouacs....

Monday [May 12] P.M. While I write the 2nd dragoon band is serenading & about 50 others are playing tattoo at various distances—a

---

2. Someone who secedes as the Confederates did from the Union; a secessionist.

grand sound this lovely moonlight night. My camp is at an old frame church in a grove—I differ from most of the Generals in preferring a tent to a house—I hope not to sleep in a house again until I see you....

Are you satisfied now with my bloodless victories? Even the abolitionists seem to be coming around—judging at least from the very handsome Resolution offered by Mr. Lovejoy in the House. I look upon that Resolution as one of the most complimentary I know of—& that too offered by my bitterest prosecutors—but to have it recognized that I have saved the lives of my men & won success by my own efforts is to me the height of glory. I hope that the result in front of Richmond will cause still greater satisfaction to the country. I still hope that the God who has been so good to me will continue to smile upon our cause, and enable me to bring this war to a speedy close, so that I may at last have the rest I want so much....

I do need rest—you know I have had but little in my life. But the will of God be done—what is given me to do I will try to do with all my might....

I think one more battle here will finish the work. I expect a great one but feel that confidence in my men & that trust in God which makes me very sanguine as to the result. They will fight me in front of Richmond I am confident—defeat there is certain destruction to them & I think will prove the ruin of their wretched cause. They are concentrating everything for the last death struggle—my government, alas, is not giving me any aid! But I will do the best I can with what I have & trust to God's mercy and the courage of my men for the result....

We march in the morning for Cumberland—gradually drawing nearer to Richmond.

General McClellan knew that the Confederate forces under Joseph Johnston had arrived in the area of Williamsburg to reinforce the small southern brigades that were stationed on the Peninsula. When Mac therefore learned that the Union army had broken through the garrison at Williamsburg, he ordered a division under General Franklin to sail up the York River in order to get behind and entrap Johnston's retreating forces. Franklin's troops reached the tip of the York River and engaged the retreating Confederates at West Point. A small but bloody skirmish was fought at West Point which lasted until about two o'clock in the afternoon. Neither side suffered major damage and the Union forces were able to hold their ground near West Point with support coming from gunboats in the York River. In spite of this engagement, however, the Confederates under Johnston were able to continue their retreat unmolested.

Federal commanders Winfield Scott Hancock (*left*) and William F. Smith (*center*) led the fight at Williamsburg, and John Newton (*right*) helped to capture West Point.

In the meanwhile, Mac was leading his army at Williamsburg in a northerly direction so as to link up with General Franklin's men at West Point.

While Mac was on his way to West Point, he received the welcome news that the pesky Confederate ironclad *Merrimack* had finally been destroyed. Now the Union navy would be able to support the Army of the Potomac from either the James or the York Rivers without fear of having ships blown out of the water. During this same period, Union forces from Fort Monroe were able to successfully assault and capture the strategic Confederate naval port at Norfolk.

The authorities in Richmond were beginning to get somewhat anxious in the face of the growing Union victories so close to their doorstep. Some Confederate officials began to openly talk about the possibility of moving their capital city to another location, which only served to stir up more panic among the citizens of Richmond.

Union Pontoon Bridge Across the James River

It was becoming only too clear that a major battle would need to be initiated by General Joseph Johnston's army if the Union advance was to be halted outside of the Confederate capital. The fact that significant battles needed to be fought around Richmond did not take anyone, least of all George McClellan, by surprise.

A telegram was sent to McClellan from the Secretary of War on May 18 directing him to move a portion of his army north of Richmond to support and resupply the Union forces under General McDowell. This directive forced Mac to divide his army on both sides of the Chickahominy River and also necessitated the time consuming task of building extra pontoon bridges across this waterway. This new line of operations also slowed and greatly complicated General McClellan's ability to supply and communicate with his scattered armies. By far, however, the most damaging aspect of this new placement of troops centered on the fact that the army of the Potomac would be much more vulnerable to attack in its divided condition. As usual, McClellan would simply have to improvise and adapt to these changes to his battle plan.

On May 19, McClellan reached the Chickahominy due east of Richmond at a crossing called Bottom's Bridge. Upon seeing that the bridge at this location was damaged, he immediately ordered his engineers to rebuild this structure. The bridge was rebuilt in under forty-eight hours, and Mac ordered several corps to cross over this bridge in the direction of Richmond. At the same time, General McClellan sent the right wing of his army well northward to capture the town and bridge at Mechanicsville. While Mac was moving a portion of his army toward Mechanicsville, General McDowell was preparing to take his division of 35,000 men in a southerly direction so they could link up with McClellan's forces for a grand assault on Richmond.

As the long-delayed attack on Richmond was finally beginning to fall into place, an unexpected storm was about to arise in the Shenandoah Valley and break out in a fury in the direction of Washington. This "storm" was provided by none other than Thomas J. Jackson, as he led a Confederate force of 10,000 men north to attack the poorly emplaced Union forces at Front Royal. The Union troops in this sector were under the command of General Banks who was responsible for guarding Washington.

General Robert E. Lee

Stonewall Jackson first received his orders from Robert E. Lee on May 17. Lee wrote:

> Whatever move you make against Banks, do it speedily, and if successful drive him toward the Potomac and create the impression, as far as possible, that you design threatening that line.

Lee and Jackson both knew how fearful Lincoln was for the safety of Washington. This particular movement was the first of several campaigns designed by Lee and Jackson to keep the Union Army off balance and distracted. As you might expect, this maneuver worked quite well, for Lincoln ordered McDowell's army of 35,000 men to return to the Valley to reinforce Banks. Once again, McClellan's troops were alone before Richmond and about to fight a major battle with Joseph Johnston outside Richmond.

On May 31, the Army of the Potomac engaged the Confederate forces east of Richmond at a town called Fair Oaks. Cannon balls and bullets flew through the air for hours as brother fought brother in mortal combat. This sharp but brief battle brought McClellan's men within six miles of the Confederate capital. The Union scouts could hear the church bells ringing in the city; nevertheless, it would be yet another case of so close and yet so far. Although this battle resulted in some progress for the North and the wounding of General Joseph Johnston, it also elevated Robert E. Lee to the position of commander of the Army of Northern Virginia.

In the Providence of God, Robert E. Lee was put into the position where he could take the Confederate army to heights it would never have reached under the capable but cautious Joseph Johnston. Lee was blessed with several days in which to plan his first real battle as field commander, due to an increasing amount of rainy weather that stalled the advancing Union forces at Fair Oaks. As McClellan and his men waited for the weather to cooperate, Lee moved his troops into position for a major offensive against Mac's supply and communication lines. By the time Lee was ready to attack, he would also be joined by Thomas "Stonewall" Jackson who managed to return safely from his campaign in the Shenandoah Valley.

As the rain soaked everything and everyone, General McClellan wrote a letter to his beloved wife on June 10 saying:

To Mary Ellen McClellan

[New Bridge] June 10 [1862] 7:30 A.M.

It is again raining hard & has been for several hours! I feel almost discouraged—that is I would do so did I not feel that it must all be for the best, & that God has some just purpose in view through all this. It is certain that there has not been for years & years such a season—it does not come by chance. I am quite checked with water so that I cannot establish safe communication over it—then again the ground is so muddy that we cannot use our artillery—the guns sink up to their axle trees. I regret at this extremely—but take comfort for the thought that God will not leave so great a struggle as this to mere chance—if he ever interferes with the destinies of men & nations this would seem to be a fit occasion for it.

Whenever I feel discouraged by adverse circumstances, I do my best to fall back on this great source of confidence & almost always find that it gives me strength to bear up against anything that may occur. I do not see how anyone can fill such a position as I do without being constantly forced to think of higher things & the Supreme Being. The great responsibility—the feeling of personal weakness & incompetency—of entire dependence on the will of God—the thousand circumstances entirely beyond our control that may defeat our best laid plans—the sight of poor human suffering—all these things will force the mind to seek rest above....

I feel quite well today—by far better than at any time before—I think that if I can stand the test of this rainy day all must be right. I will not go out while it rains if I can help it....

The Spaniards are still here, & I fear will remain some time unless this rain drives them off. Prim is very well, but it is a nuisance to be obliged to be polite when one's head is full of more important things....

Still raining very hard—I don't know what will become of us!

As the month of June pressed on, General Joe Johnston was struggling to recover from his serious chest and shoulder wound. He would be out of action for an extended period. Johnston's replacement, Robert E. Lee, was busy formulating an aggressive battle plan with the help of his first-string Generals Longstreet and Hill. Due to the hard fighting of McClellan's men, Lee and his forces were now up

General A. P. Hill

against the proverbial wall of their own capital. In spite of the fact that Lee was outnumbered, he managed to make up for this deficiency by way of sheer audacity and boldness. General Lee threw the West Point strategy manual aside as he ordered his men to position. The circumstances would not allow Lee to be conservative. He would make up new rules for military strategy and in the process would forever write his name on the role of great military leaders.

Field Hospital after the Battle of Fair Oaks

While both armies tried to assemble their forces for the next battle, the field hospitals on both sides were already reporting a brisk business in the aftermath of the battle of Fair Oaks or, as the Confederates call it, Seven Pines. Two miles behind the

Federal Lines a field hospital was set up at Savage's Station. Chaplain J. J. Marks describes some of what he saw at this medical outpost.

> During the entire night the wounded were brought in, until they covered the grounds around the house of Mr. Savage, and filled all the outhouses, barns, and sheds. Lying alongside of our wounded were many Confederate soldiers and officers.... The rebels were uniformly treated as kindly as the Union soldiers. All night the surgeons were occupied in amputations; and... they found it impossible to look after those whose condition demanded the immediate administration of food and stimulants to revive them. Wounded men suffer greatly from cold, and shiver as in winter, or with an ague.[3] It was therefore essential to lift them from the damp ground and cover them as far as possible. In the course of the evening twenty or thirty soldiers from different regiments, who had borne in upon their shoulders their wounded comrades, permitted me to organize them into a corps of nurses. Colonel [Samuel] McKelvy, who was more active than any other for the relief of our men, furnished twenty bales of hay, a thousand blankets, and permitted me to draw on the commissary Department for coffee, sugar, and crackers to an indefinite amount. The nurse-soldiers soon spread down this hay, and many a shivering, wounded man, when lifted from the damp earth and placed upon the soft grass bed with a blanket spread over him, poured out his gratitude in a thousand blessings. When this was done we followed with hot coffee, and found our way to every suffering man. Everywhere we were compelled to place our feet in streams of blood. One spectacle of anguish and agony only succeeded another. The mind was overwhelmed and benumbed by such scenes of accumulated misery.... Great must be the cause which demands such a sacrifice.

> Here and there over the grounds were seen through that night a circle of lanterns waving around the tables of amputators. Every few moments there was a shriek of some poor fellow under the knife. And one after another the sufferers were brought forward and laid down before the surgeons on stretchers, each waiting his

---

3. A fever, usually malarial, that is marked by regularly recurring chills.

turn. After the crude procedure, each victim possessed a face as white as marble and every line telling that he had passed through a suffering the utmost which human nature could endure. Each man was borne away and laid down for some kindhearted nurse to pour into his lips a few drops of brandy... and give him the assurance of life and sympathy. There a brother knelt and wept over a dying brother.... There a father held up in his arms a dying son and was receiving his last message to mother, sister, and brother. Here a group of sympathizing soldiers stood around a dying companion who was loudly bewailing his early death, and that he should never again see his native hills. There four or five were holding in their strong arms one whose brain, having been pierced with a ball and deprived of reason, was strong in the frantic energy of madness. Here a beckoning hand urged me to come and ... sit down by [a sufferer's] side and tell him what he must do to be saved.... Another begged me to come early in the morning and write a line to father or wife. Others entreated that they should not be compelled to submit to the knife of the operator but that their limbs might be spared them.... Others begged that some board might bear their names and be placed at the head of their graves....

At one place where a wounded soldier was panting his last I was summoned. He begged me to pray for him, and, taking from his finger a gold ring, he asked me to send it to his wife, who had given it to him on the day of their marriage.... In a few minutes the last battle was fought, and the soldier was asleep.... In another group of sufferers I found a little boy apparently not more than twelve years of age. The long hair thrown back from a beautiful forehead enabled me to see by the lantern light a very childlike face. His right leg had been amputated above his knee, and he was lying motionless and apparently breathless, and as white as snow. I bent over him and put my fingers on his wrist, and discovered to my surprise a faint trembling of pulse. I immediately said to my attendant, 'Why, this child is alive!' 'Yes, sir,' said he, opening his eyes, 'I am alive. Will you not send me to my mother?' 'And where is your mother,' said I, 'my child?' 'In Sumterville, South Carolina,' he replied. 'Oh, yes, my son! We will certainly send you to your mother.' 'Well, well,' said he, 'that is kind. I will go to sleep now.'

On the Sabbath morning of June 1st, I saw Generals Keyes and Heintzelman leave the headquarters of the latter at Savage's Station. They rode, surrounded by their aides, across the field leading to the Williamsburg Road [which coursed toward Richmond]. I had heard during the night that a hospital had been created about a mile from the Station towards the battlefield. I started to find it, and in a short time reached the house, in and around which were lying a multitude of our dying and wounded.... Ambulances were here removing the disabled to Savage's Station. Mingled with the great number of wounded were many dead, who, having been brought in, did not survive the night....

Quite a few of the soldiers who fought during the Peninsular Campaign saw the dark side of war. The dark side of the war is just that, dark and ugly. There is no honest way to dress it up to look nice. Towards the end of the War Between the States, Robert E. Lee would utter these truthful remarks, "It is well that war is so terrible or we should grow too fond of it."

Men like Lee and McClellan would see a lot of ugly battlefield schemes before their time in the saddle was over.

Although George McClellan was not in a field hospital in May or early June, he probably should have been. During these weeks, he was often bedridden, or should I say cot ridden, with his old Mexican disease—malaria. By mid-June, General McClellan was well enough to take brief rides on his horse again. While Mac was in the saddle inspecting his troops around Richmond, a Confederate horseman named J. E. B. Stuart was blazing a trail of glory by riding with his cavalry regiment totally around McClellan's positions. Stuart, a cavalry general, was on a special reconnaissance mission for Robert E. Lee and was sent to locate the exact position of Federal supply and communication stations. News of this daring and successful exploit reached newspapers in the North and South and was an unwelcomed source of embarrassment for George McClellan. He did not need another headache at this critical hour.

On June 22, the rains finally stopped and the roads around Richmond began to dry. McClellan ordered the divisions of his army on the southern side of the Chickahominy River to advance in stages toward Richmond stopping first at Seven Pines and proceeding on to the Old Tavern crossroads. General McClellan was hoping to establish the first of several siege positions at Old Tavern and bombard Richmond into submission. He had not totally ruled out the notion of a grand assault on the Confederate capital at this time, but recent intelligence reports continued to lead Mac to believe that a frontal assault on Richmond would be too costly.

General Heintzelman moved his Union corps forward on Wednesday, June 25, and was met by a powerful Confederate force who immediately went on the attack. The brief but intense battle was at a place called Oak Grove and was to be the first of seven days worth of aggressive fighting around Richmond. Historians have cleverly labeled this period as the Seven Days' Battles. The first day of fighting was not tremendously significant, but the day ended with the Union forces commanding the battlefield, so in one key sense the battle was a victory for McClellan's men.

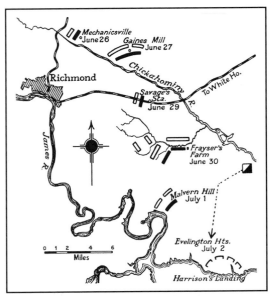

Map of Seven Days Battle

At the opening of the Seven Days' battles, the Army of Northern Virginia under Lee had 85,000 men in the field. This included the 17,000 men who were under the command of Thomas Jackson. The Army of the Potomac had 104,000 men ready for battle. In the opening phase of the Confederate offensive, Lee would endeavor to successfully turn the right wing of McClellan's army that was posted on the north side of the Chickahominy River. If Lee's men could outflank the Federal troops in the North, they might well be able to cutoff or capture the main Union supply depot at White House and perhaps disrupt the rail line that brought supplies to McClellan's men.

The second day of fighting was once again initiated by Lee at the town of Mechanicsville and eventually wound up at a swampy area off the Chickahominy called Beaver Dam Creek. The assault came against Union General Porter whose men were well positioned and entrenched. In much the same manner as the first day of fighting, the Confederates fought hard but were ultimately repulsed with heavy losses. Upon hearing of the outcome of the first two days of battle, Mac joyfully praised his men. He telegraphed the Secretary of War stating, "Victory of today complete and against great odds. I almost begin to think we are invincible."

The battle plan of Lee shifted on the morning of the twenty-seventh, he ordered General Prince John Magruder to make several probing movements on the center of the Union line situated south of the Chickahominy. These movements, along with an assault by Thomas Jackson's forces who were near the James River, were designed to mislead McClellan into believing that his army was being assaulted on all fronts. In the confusion, Lee resumed his attack upon General Porter's men, who had reformed their line at a place called Gaines Mill. This time, it was the Federal troops who were forced to retreat as the Confederates were able to push back their stubborn enemy. From all accounts, the nine hours of fighting at Gaines Mill was the fiercest and bloodiest of the campaign. Thousands of men died on both sides of the battlefield.

From McClellan's perspective, the fighting in the North was going so poorly that he must either attack Richmond in force or consolidate his forces south of the Chickahominy and change his supply base from White House to Harrison's Landing on the James River. The weary young General decided during the late morning of June 28 to place his army in retreat toward the James and away from

Richmond. Lee's offensive had cost his army dearly in respect to casualties, but it had accomplished what had to be done to save the Confederate capital. Most importantly for Lee, the manner in which the battle was perceived by McClellan and most of his generals, would only serve to perpetuate the long-standing myth that the Confederate Army of Northern Virginia was larger than the Army of the Potomac.

As the Army of the Potomac began its organized retreat towards the James River, its general was not exactly in a fine humor. George McClellan had the same cheery outlook as a young child who has just had Christmas canceled. He simply could not believe that his grand campaign to capture Richmond was slowly slipping through his hands. If nothing else, he had to set the record straight as to who was responsible for this human tragedy. With this thought in mind, General McClellan sat down and wrote a choice letter to Stanton and the President stating:

> *To Edwin M. Stanton*
>
> *Savage Station June 28 [1862] 12:20 A.M.*
>
> *I now know the full history of the day [June 27]. On this side of the river—the right bank—we repulsed several very strong attacks. On the left bank our men did all that men could do, all that soldiers could accomplish— but they were overwhelmed by vastly superior numbers even after I brought my last reserves into action. The loss on both sides is terrible—I believe it will prove to be the most desperate battle of the war. The sad remnants of my men behave as men—those battalions who fought most bravely & suffered most are still in the best order. My regulars were superb & I count upon what are left to turn another battle in company with their gallant comrades of the Volunteers. Had I (20,000) twenty thousand or even (10,000) ten thousand fresh troops to use tomorrow I could take Richmond, but I have not a man in reserve & shall be glad to cover my retreat & save the material & personnel of the Army.*
>
> *If we have lost the day we have yet preserved our honor & no one need blush for the Army of the Potomac. I have lost this battle because my*

force was too small. I again repeat that I am not responsible for this &
I say it with the earnestness of a General who feels in his heart the loss
of every brave man who has been needlessly sacrificed today. I still hope
to retrieve our fortunes, but to do this the Govt. must view the matter
in the same earnest light that I do—you must send me very large rein-
forcements, & send them at once.

I shall draw back to this side of the Chickahominy & think I can with-
draw all our material. Please understand that in this battle we have
lost nothing but men & those the best we have.

In addition to what I have already said I only wish to say to the Presdt
that I think he is wrong, in regarding me as ungenerous when I said
that my force was too weak. I merely reiterated a truth which today has
been too plainly proved. I should have gained this battle with (10,000)
ten thousand fresh men. If at this instant I could dispose of (10,000)
ten thousand fresh men I could gain the victory tomorrow.

I know that a few thousand more men would have changed this battle
from a defeat to a victory—as it is the Govt must not & cannot hold
me responsible for the result.

I feel too earnestly tonight—I have seen too many dead & wounded
comrades to feel otherwise than that the Govt has not sustained this
Army. If you do not do so now the game is lost.

If I save this Army now I tell you plainly that I owe no thanks to you or
any other persons in Washington—you have done your best to sacrifice
this Army.

Geo. B. McClellan

George McClellan reached the James on June 29 consumed with
a hundred issues related to how to reorganize his new base of operations. McClellan's Chief of Staff, Randolph Marcy moved Mac's
headquarters to Haxall's Landing on the James as ordered. The
Army of the Potomac was retreating along a marshy line known as
the White Oak swamp, fighting skirmishes as they moved southeast
of Richmond. Late on the twenty-ninth, Union troops began to
establish a key defensive position at Malvern Hill in order to slow or

stop the Confederate forces who were attacking them and their supply trains. Malvern Hill was located about twenty miles southeast of the Confederate capital.

While a large Union force was digging in at Malvern Hill, Mac and his staff were miles away at Haxall's Landing boarding the gunboat *Galena*. Early that evening, Captain John Rodgers steamed up the James with George McClellan to bombard the Confederate columns who were making their way towards Malvern Hill.

On June 30, Lee once again attacked the Federal troops stationed at the town of Glendale. These troops were trying to protect the rear of the retreating Union army. It was the Confederates last desperate effort to cutoff and destroy the northern wing of the Army of the Potomac. With commander McClellan preoccupied on the James or at Malvern Hill, the Union forces at Glendale had to rely upon their own courage and initiative to keep themselves from being destroyed. By the grace of God, the Army of the Potomac was able to escape the final push of the defenders of Richmond and avoid a rout of their army. The army of General Lee would soon pull back toward Richmond for rest and repair.

For reasons that historians and military analysts can not comprehend, General McClellan chose to spend the final days of the Seven Days' Battle on board the *Galena* or at his headquarters at Haxall's Landing. Some historians have gone so far as to accuse Mac of being a coward for hiding out in a naval vessel while his troops were fighting a vicious pitched battle only miles away. Although it is impossible to say precisely why Mac spent so much time on board a gunboat at this particular period, it is certainly safe to say that, whatever else he may have been, McClellan was no coward. It is a well established fact that George McClellan routinely exposed himself, sometimes foolishly, to enemy fire as he commanded his troops in the field.

By the end of the first week in July, Mac had established a secure position at Harrison's Landing as his new base of operations twenty-six miles from Richmond. This location was right on the James River which made it quite suitable as a place to receive the vast amount of supplies that were needed each day by McClellan's huge army. Mac had regained enough of his equilibrium by this point to write his wife on July 6 the following:

To Mary Ellen McClellan

[Berkeley] July 6 [1862] Sunday 2:15 A.M.

Early in the evening [July 5] I received the intelligence that secesh was in full force in front of me. I have just completed my arrangements to meet him & believe that with God's blessing we will defeat him terribly. I go into this battle with the full conviction that our honor makes it necessary for me to share the fate of my army. My men are confident & I have no doubt as to our success unless the Creator orders otherwise. I believe we will give them a tremendous thrashing & I still hope that from my universal anxieties I will yet find repose—may God grant it thus! Whatever the result may be I am sure that you will never have cause to blush for me—therefore my conscience is quite clear—God has done far more for me than I had any right to expect—I trust, most humbly, that unworthy as I am he will not desert me now. I yet believe that there is in store for us the supreme happiness of being together once more. If this cannot be in this world, I trust I may be forgiven for my many faults & sins & be permitted to rejoin in Heaven the one who has made my life so happy....

Tomorrow [July 6] will probably determine the fate of the country—I expect to be attacked by greatly superior numbers & hope to beat them.

Mac had already wired Lincoln in early July requesting fifty thousand fresh troops so he could renew his offensive against Richmond. The President told him: "The idea of sending you fifty thousand, or any other considerable force, promptly, is simply absurd.... If you think you are not strong enough to take Richmond just now, I do not ask you to try just now. Save the Army, material, and personnel; and I will strengthen it for the offensive again, as fast as I can."

President Lincoln was so distraught by the events on the Peninsula that he decided to sail down the Chesapeake and visit with his embittered general at Harrison's Landing. The brief meeting of these two leaders on July 8 accomplished little, as both men endeavored to bear up under the sweltering Virginia sun. Before Lincoln sailed back to Washington, however, Mac would provide him with a letter detailing his recommendations for a successful war policy for the nation. As usual, the President would ignore most of Mac's advice in the months ahead. The letter to the President stated:

To Abraham Lincoln

(Confidential) Head Quarters, Army of the Potomac

Mr. President Camp near Harrison's Landing, Va., July 7, 1862

You have been fully informed, that the Rebel army is in our front, with the purpose of overwhelming us by attacking our positions or reducing us by blocking our river communications. I cannot but regard our condition as critical and I earnestly desire, in view of possible contingencies, to lay before your Excellency, for your private consideration, my general views concerning the existing state of the rebellion; although they do not strictly relate to the situation of this Army or strictly come within the scope of my official duties. These views amount to convictions and are deeply impressed upon my mind and heart.

Our cause must never be abandoned; it is the cause of free institutions and self government. The Constitution and the Union must be preserved, whatever may be the cost in time, treasure, and blood. If secession is successful, other dissolutions are clearly to be seen in the future. Let neither military disaster, political faction or foreign war shake your settled purpose to enforce the equal operations of the laws of the United States upon the people of every state.

The time has come when the Government must determine upon a civil and military policy, covering the whole ground of our national trouble. The responsibility of determining, declaring, and supporting such civil and military policy, and of directing the whole course of national affairs in regard to the rebellion, must now be assumed and exercised by you or our cause will be lost. The constitution gives you power sufficient even for the present terrible exigency.

This rebellion has assumed the character of a War; as such it should be regarded; and it should be conducted upon the highest principles known to Christian Civilization. It should not be a War looking to the subjugation of the people of any state, in any event. It should not be, at all, a War upon population; but against armed forces and political organizations. Neither confiscation of property, political executions of persons, territorial organization of states or forcible abolition of slavery should be contemplated for a moment. In prosecuting the War, all private property and unarmed persons should be strictly protected; subject only to the necessities of military operations. All private property taken for military use should be paid or receipted for; pillage and waste should be treated as high crimes; all unnecessary trespass sternly prohibited; and offensive demeanor by the military towards citizens promptly rebuked. Military arrests should not be tolerated, except in places where active hostilities exist; and oaths not required by enactments—Constitutionally made—should be neither demanded nor received. Military government should be confined to the preservation of public order and the protection of political rights.

Military power should not be allowed to interfere with the relations of servitude, either by supporting or impairing the authority of the master; except for repressing disorder as in other cases. Slaves contraband under the Act of Congress, seeking military protection, should receive it. The right of the Government to appropriate permanently to its own service claims to slave labor should be asserted and the right of the owner to compensation therefore should be recognized. This principle might be extended upon grounds of military necessity and security to all the slaves within a particular state; thus working manumission in such state—and in Missouri, perhaps in Western Virginia also, and possibly even in Maryland—the expediency of such a military measure is only a question of time. A system of policy thus constitutional and conservative, and pervaded by the influences of Christianity and freedom, would receive the support of almost all truly loyal men, would deeply impress the rebel masses and all foreign nations, and it might be humbly hoped that it would commend itself to the favor of the Almighty. Unless the principles governing the further conduct of our struggle shall be made known and approved, the effort to obtain requisite forces will be almost hopeless. A declaration of radical views, especially upon slavery, will rapidly disintegrate our present Armies.

The policy of the Government must be supported by concentrations of military power. The national forces should not be dispersed in expeditions, posts of occupation and numerous Armies; but should be mainly collected into masses and brought to bear upon the Armies of the Confederate States; those Armies thoroughly defeated, the political structure which they support would soon cease to exist.

In carrying out any system of policy which you may form, you will require a Commander-in-Chief of the Army; one who possesses your confidence, understands your views and who is competent to execute your orders by directing the military forces of the Nation to the accomplishment of the objects by you proposed. I do not ask that place for myself. I am willing to serve you in such position as you may assign me and I will do so as faithfully as ever subordinate served superior.

I may be on the brink of eternity and as I hope forgiveness from my maker I have written this letter with sincerity towards you and from love for my country.

> *Very respectfully your obdt svt,*
>
> *Geo. B. McClellan*
> *Maj. Gen'l Comd'g*

His Excellency A Lincoln
Presdt U.S.

President Lincoln read the lengthy and heartfelt letter from McClellan during his visit to the Peninsula. After he was finished, the President simply thanked the general for his thoughts, and without further comment, put the letter in his pocket.

No sooner had President Lincoln returned to Washington, when he began to put plans into motion to return the Army of the Potomac to Washington. While Mac sat a few miles from Richmond, his commander-in-chief was busy doing exactly what General McClellan advised him not to do.

The mind-set of Lincoln as he returned to the White House must not have been a total mystery to George McClellan, for he wrote a letter to the President on July 12 urging him to keep the Army of the Potomac near Richmond. Mac wrote:

To Abraham Lincoln

[TELEGRAM]

Berkerkey July 12 [1862] 7:15 A.M.

Hill and Longstreet crossed into New Kent County via Long Bridge. I am still ignorant what road they afterwards took but will know shortly. Nothing else of interest since last dispatch.

Rain ceased & everything quiet. Men resting well, but beginning to be impatient for another fight.

I am more and more convinced that this Army ought not to be withdrawn from here—but promptly reinforced & thrown again upon Richmond. If we have a little more than half a chance we can take it. I dread the effects of any retreat upon the morale of the men.

Geo. B. McClellan
Major Gen'l Comd'g

The young Napoleon also wrote his wife at this time, expressing the optimistic view that, "I still hope to get to Richmond this summer, unless the government commits some extraordinarily idiotic act." In addition, Mac confided in his wife that he understood that his predicament was totally under the control of Almighty God.

My conscience is clear—I have done the best I could—God disposed of events as to Him seemed best. I submit to His decrees with perfect cheerfulness, [and] as sure as He rules I believe that all will yet be for the best....

How I have longed to see you in the midst of my troubles. The thought of you has been an immense consolation [and] support to me. How perfectly happy I shall be if God sees fit to permit me to be with you once more. I will never leave you again if it is in the power of humanity to avoid it. Nor rank, nor wealth, nor honors can reconcile me to absence from you.

It was not long before George McClellan began to hear that Lincoln was preparing to bring Major General Henry Halleck from the western theater to Washington so he could assume the post of general-in-chief of the army. This intelligence turned out to be correct as Halleck officially assumed command of the Union armies on July 23. From the first time that Mac heard of Halleck's appointment, he knew that Lincoln was poised to recall the Army of the Potomac from Richmond and possibly to relieve him from command. McClellan shared his views on these issues with his wife during one of his routine letters:

To Mary Ellen McClellan

July 18 [1862] Berkeley Friday 9:00 P.M.

…I have my head half occupied with the idea of making another last appeal to the Presdt to endeavor to beat some sense into his head.…

I am inclined now to think that the Presdt will make Halleck comdr of the Army & that the first pretext will be seized to supersede me in command of this army—their game seems to be to withhold reinforcements & then to relieve me for not advancing—well knowing that I have not the means to do so. If they supersede me in command of the Army of the Potomac I will resign my commission at once; if they appoint Halleck Comd'g Gen'l I will remain in command of this army as long as they will allow me to, provided the army is in danger & likely to play an active part. I cannot remain as a subordinate in the army I once commanded any longer than the interests of my own Army of the Potomac require. I owe no gratitude to any but my own soldiers here—none to the Govt or to the country. I have done my best for my country—I expect nothing in return—they are my debtors, not I theirs.…

My letter to Stanton was fairly "diplomatic" & if you read it carefully you will see that it is bitter enough—politely expressed, but containing much more than is on the surface.…

If things come to pass as I anticipate I shall leave the service with a sad heart for my country, but a light one for myself. I am tired of being dependent on men I despise from the bottom of my heart. I cannot express to you the infinite contempt I feel for these people; but one thing keeps me at my work—love for my country & my army. Surely no General ever had better cause to love his men than I have to love mine.

Unhappily the men are too often better than their officers.

As the estranged general from Philadelphia contemplated his future he also took advantage of the lull in fighting to visit numerous Union field hospitals. This action only served to strengthen the already strong bonds that existed between Mac and his fighting men. He told his friend,

> I can't tell you how glad I am that I went to see all those poor wounded men yesterday. Another batch will come tonight, [and] I will if possible go to see all of them tomorrow morning. I regard it as a duty I owe the poor fellows—rather a hard one to perform, but still one that cannot be neglected. I am sorry that no other General officer does the same—it would do the men good....

As the month of July wound down, the politicians at Washington were struggling to put the best face on their military woes. The Peninsula Campaign had already cost the government over 100 million dollars and the costs to sustain the giant army under McClellan were continuing to mount. Notwithstanding these important issues, the move to recall McClellan and possibly replace him from command was fraught with political and military danger. Perhaps the greatest concern of the politicians was the effect that Mac's dismissal would have upon the morale of the Army of the Potomac who nearly worshipped their general. This of course, was a very real problem. Many in Washington, including Lincoln, seriously wondered if McClellan's dismissal would result in a general mutiny and subsequent march to seize the government.

One of General Halleck's first moves was to establish a new Army of Virginia under the command of General John Pope. This army would be placed south of Washington and would be reinforced for a prompt attack upon the Confederates who were in the vicinity of the old Bull Run battlefield. Not surprisingly, Halleck ordered McClellan in early August to close down his operation on the Peninsula so his army could be brought up to reinforce the troops fighting near Washington under General Pope.

The Lincoln administration cleverly bypassed the problem of dismissing Mac outright by keeping him in charge of the Army of the Potomac in a symbolic sense. While at the same time placing his troops on semi-permanent "loan" to General Pope. By mid-August General McClellan would, for all practical purposes, be a commander without an army.

George McClellan appealed the decision of Lincoln and Halleck to no avail. He told his wife on August 14 that this recall order caused him "the greatest pain I ever experienced.... We are not going to Richmond but to Fort Monroe, I am ashamed to say!... It is a terrible blow to me, but I have done all that could be done to prevent it, without success, so I must submit as best I can and carry it out."

General "Stonewall" Jackson

During Mac's appeal to General Halleck, he attempted to warn him about Pope's inability to deal with the shrewd and aggressive troops commanded by Thomas "Stonewall" Jackson. "He will suddenly appear when least expected," stated Mac in a prophetic moment. Privately, General McClellan told his commanders that the proud and arrogant John Pope would probably "be in full retreat or badly whipped within a week."

Transports on the Potomac

It was late August before General McClellan would be able to reluctantly bring a portion of his army to a position south of Washington. The depressing scene involving the recall of one hundred thousand men from the door of Richmond, was described by a Union surgeon from New York by the name of George Stevens. He wrote:

Transports of every size and description were riding upon the bay or lashed to the wharves, and infantry, cavalry, and artillery were crowding toward the beach, ready to take their turn to embark. The scene was one of unusual activity, resembling only the one we had witnessed on embarking for the Peninsula months ago. At length all were on board, and the transports swung out upon the bay and steamed up the Potomac.... What a contrast there was in the appearance of [the] men now, compared to when they came down the river in April! Then our ranks were full; the men were healthy and in fresh vigor; their uniforms were new and clean, and their muskets and equipment were polished and glistening. Now we looked about with sadness when we remembered how many of our former companions were absent, and how few present. We could bring to mind many who went to the Peninsula full of hope who had sunk as victims of the malarial poisons and now rested in humble graves at Yorktown or along the Chickahominy; and many others who had nobly fallen upon the field of strife; and yet others who now were wearing out tedious days of sickness in hospitals or at home.

As General McClellan prepared to steam away from Fort Monroe on the *City of Hudson,* he wrote his wife on August 22 stating:

To Mary Ellen McClellan

[Fort Monroe] Aug. 22 [1862] 10:00 A.M.

...I did not get back from the Fort until sometime after midnight & too tired to write....

I shall go to the Fort pretty soon & as soon as the tents are dry move everything on board the vessels so that I shall be ready to start at a moment's notice. I have two Corps off & away.

Franklin ought to have been off nearly by this time, but he & Smith have so little energy that I fear they will be very slow about it. They have disappointed me terribly—I do not at all doubt Franklin's loyalty now, but his efficiency is very little—I am very sorry that it has turned out so. The main, perhaps the only cause is that he has been & still is sick—& one ought not to judge harshly of a person in that condition. I presume I ought also to make a great deal of allowance for Smith also on the same account—so will try to be as charitable as we can under all these circumstances. I think they are pretty well scared in Washn & probably with good reason. I am confident that the disposition to be made of me will depend entirely upon the state of their nerves in Washn. If they feel safe there I will no doubt be shelved—perhaps placed in command near vice Gen'l Dix. I don't care what they do— would not object to being kept here for a while—because I could soon get things in such condition that I could have you here with me....

Their sending for me to go to Washn only indicates a temporary alarm—if they are at all reassured you will see that they will soon get rid of me. I shall be only too happy to get back to quiet life again—for I am truly & heartily sick of the troubles I have had & am not fond of being a target for the abuse & slander of all the rascals in the country. Well, we will continue to trust in God & feel certain that all is for the best—it is often difficult to understand the ways of Providence—but I have faith enough to believe that nothing is done without some great purpose. But enough of my troubles!...

I feel so sick & tired of human nature that I am already wary of being brought in contact with it. To think that a man whom I so sincerely admired, trusted & liked as I did Stanton turning against me as he has—& that without any cause that I am aware of! Pah—it is too bad!...

On August 24, George McClellan and his staff sailed up the Potomac River and landed eleven miles northeast of the town of Fredericksburg, at a place called Aquia Landing. All of Mac's divisions had already landed at this spot days before, and were taking the quickest possible overland route to link up with the Army of Virginia and Generals Pope and Burnside.

McClellan's relief forces were not quick enough for the wily Tom Jackson, however, for he had already managed to turn up in the rear of Pope's army near Manassas. As incredible as it must have seemed to the already frustrated Union army, old Stonewall was about to smash the life out of yet another Federal force. To add insult to injury, he would do it at almost the exact location that earned him the name of Stonewall a year or so earlier—Manassas. So much for Southern hospitality!

Two corps from McClellan's relief force did eventually reach the embattled Union Army south of Washington, but their arrival did little to affect the outcome of the battle of Second Manassas. All McClellan's troops could do was to provide helpful rear guard action thereby keeping Jackson's forces from destroying great numbers of retreating Union soldiers. The now familiar scene involving long caravans of retreating blue uniforms was enough to tempt George McClellan to say I told you so. Washington was once again filled to capacity with a broken army. Who would Lincoln call upon to save Washington and his army? He would call upon the only man who had the organizational talent to make it happen—Lincoln would again summon McClellan to the capital.

Various members of Lincoln's cabinet were indignant when they received word that Mac was once again in charge of the Army of the Potomac. The radical Treasury Secretary Salmon Chase, had only recently been circulating a petition to get rid of McClellan altogether. Lincoln tried to reason with his cabinet members, that as long as General McClellan was

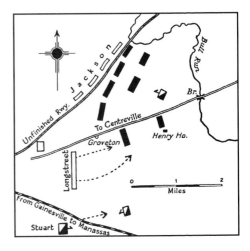

The Battle of Second Manassas

useful he would use his talents until someone better came along. This attitude ultimately became the working principle in regard to George McClellan. He was, after all, the disposable patriot.

As McClellan contemplated his newly invigorated military command around Washington, he made it clear to his wife that he viewed all of these new circumstances as being under the direction of the Lord. On September 2 Mac wrote:

To Mary Ellen McClellan

[Washington] Sept. 2 [1862] 12:30 P.M.

I was surprised this morning when at bkft by a visit from the Presdt & Halleck—in which the former expressed the opinion that the troubles now impending could be overcome better by me than anyone else. Pope is ordered to fall back upon Washn & as he re-enters everything is to come under my command again! A terrible & thankless task—yet I will do my best with God's blessing to perform it. God knows that I need his help. I am too busy to write any more now—Pray that God will help me in the great task now imposed upon me—I assume it reluctantly—with a full knowledge of all its difficulties & of the immensity of the responsibility. I only consent to take it for my country's sake & with the humble hope that God has called me to it—how I pray that he may support me!...

Don't be worried—my conscience is clear & I can trust in God.

It would have been easy for General McClellan to turn down the position offered by the officials at Washington who obviously cared nothing for him and his reputation. In spite of the obstacle of pride, however, Mac took up the calling to save Washington for the second time. He was willing to continue to serve his country, chiefly because he was committed to please God in what he considered to be his calling. Mac was finished with the business of trying to please two-faced politicians and hypocrites. He would stay with his army and its brave soldiers until he was convinced that his efforts were no longer useful to his captain—The Lord Jesus Christ.

Chapter Nine

The Conservative General

SEPTEMBER 1862

Robert E. Lee lost little time in attempting to exploit the recent Confederate victory at Manassas. He pushed a large force of fighting men across the upper Potomac into Maryland, with Stonewall Jackson's division in the lead. Whenever Lee could pick the time and place to fight the Union army, he always felt confident of victory. In the coming weeks, however, Lee's confidence would very nearly cost him his entire army.

The Maryland offensive in the fall of 1862 was calculated to force the Federal army stationed at Washington to come out of their fortified positions to engage an elite force of seasoned Confederates. The move into Maryland was also prompted by the need for the Army of Northern Virginia to forage for food and equipment in some other location than the impoverished Shenandoah Valley. Lee was hoping that the demoralized Federal army would not be able to put an effective force into the field for several weeks, or perhaps, months. This would give his troops ample time to rest and get resupplied at the expense of the farmers in a pro-union state. As we will soon see, however, a Federal army moved against Lee more quickly and powerfully than he had hoped.

It took less than a week for General McClellan to reorganize and revitalize the Army of the Potomac. He took the shattered remnants of Pope's Army of Virginia and incorporated them into his newly expanded legions. Mac now prepared to take sixteen newly formed divisions—some 85,000 men—into Maryland to destroy the southern invaders who were last seen near the town of Frederick. The transformation of the Union army was so amazing that even the disillusioned President would marvel at the administrative expertise of McClellan. Lincoln met with Mac on September 5 and gave him the authority to take the field. The President would later confess that even if McClellan could not fight successfully in an offensive campaign, "he excels in making others ready to fight."

After George McClellan met with the commander-in-chief and briefed each of his corp commanders, he wrote his wife stating:

To Mary Ellen McClellan

[Washington] Sept. 5 [1862] 11:00 A.M.

...Again I have been called upon to save the country—the case is desperate, but with God's help I will try unselfishly to do my best & if He wills it accomplish the salvation of the nation. My men are true & will stand by me to the last. I still hope for success & will leave nothing undone to gain it....

How weary I am of this struggle against adversity. But one thing sustains me—& that is my trust in God—I know that the interests at stake are so great as to justify His interference—not for me, but for the innocent thousands, millions rather, who have been plunged in misery by no fault of theirs. It is probable that our communications will be cut off in a day or two—but don't be worried. You may rest assured that I am doing all I can for my country & that no shame shall rest upon you willfully brought upon you by me....

My hands are full, so is my heart....

4 P.M. ...It makes my heart bleed to see the poor shattered remnants of my noble Army of the Potomac, poor fellows! and to see how they love me even now. I hear them calling out to me as I ride among them— "George—don't leave us again!" "They shan't take you away from us again." etc. etc. I can hardly restrain myself when I see how fearfully they are reduced in numbers & realize how many of them lie unburied on the field of battle where their lives were uselessly sacrificed. It is the most terrible trial I ever experienced—Truly God is trying me in the fire....

By September 8, General McClellan had established a field headquarters at Rockville, Maryland about fourteen miles northwest of
the capital. Experience had taught the general not to overstay his
welcome at Washington, therefore, he moved his impressive army
toward the city of Frederick with the intention of striking Lee in
short order. Little did General McClellan realize that he would soon
be in possession of a copy of the entire Confederate plan for the
Maryland campaign.

While the Army of the Potomac marched through the beautiful
rolling hills of the Maryland countryside, Lee felt confident enough
to divide his force of 40,000 troops into three major units. One of
the Confederate units under the command of Stonewall Jackson was
sent to capture the Union supply station at Harper's Ferry. Another
force was sent by General Lee to occupy the town of Boonsboro and
would provide rear guard protection for the Confederate army. The
last major contingent of Southern troops located near Frederick,
Maryland would, naturally, be commanded by Lee himself.

The bold plan of General Lee, was intended to permit him to
capture the key Union installation at Harper's Ferry before McClellan's host could react to this unexpected maneuver. Robert E. Lee
was quite sure that Thomas Jackson could surprise the Federal division at Harper's Ferry and still be back in time to help the reunited
Confederate army clobber McClellan. There was, however, one tiny
circumstance that Lee could not envision in his clever plan.

On September 13, as Mac's army entered Frederick, an official
copy of Lee's entire battle plan was brought into his headquarters.
These valuable documents were found in a nearby field by a Union
soldier, wrapped around three cigars. Suddenly, the entire military
landscape had changed for McClellan. He was no longer blindly
moving toward a Confederate force that he believed was larger than
his own. Mac was now the master of a large army hungry for victory,
and fully understood that Lee's army was hopelessly divided and vulnerable to attack. Lee's only remaining advantage was that General
McClellan was still unaware of how small the Confederate army in
Maryland was at this time.

General McClellan sent off a telegram to President Lincoln informing him of the disposition of his army and alerting him to the fact that he had possession of the plans of the enemy. Mac wrote:

To Abraham Lincoln

2:35 A.M. [TELEGRAM]

To the President Hd Qrs Frederick Sept. 13th [1862] 12:00 M.

I have the whole Rebel force in front of me but am confident and no time shall be lost. I have a difficult task to perform but with God's blessing will accomplish it. I think Lee has made a gross mistake and that he will be severely punished for it. The Army is in motion as rapidly as possible. I hope for a great success if the plans of the Rebels remain unchanged. We have possession of Cotocktane. I have all the plans of the Rebels and will catch them in their own trap if my men are equal to the emergency. I now feel that I can count on them as of old. All forces of Pennsylvania should be placed to cooperate at Chambersburg. My respects to Mrs. Lincoln.

Received most enthusiastically by the ladies. Will send you trophies. All well and with God's Blessing will accomplish it.

Geo. B. McClellan

George McClellan ordered his division commanders to ready their troops for a rapid march the following morning toward the center of Lee's scattered armies. Mac told his old West Point classmate, John Gibbon, "Tomorrow we will pitch into his center and if you people will only do two good, hard days' marching I will put Lee in a position he will find hard to get out of."

Early in the morning of September 14, the young Napoleon marched his men aggressively up the slopes toward South Mountain. He put Generals Reno and Sturgis at the command of the left wing of his advancing forces. Mac's main attack was toward Middletown at Turner's Gap one mile north of South Mountain. The Army of the Potomac desperately needed to break through the region around South Mountain so these troops could cut the Confederate army in two and deny Lee the opportunity to reunite his already outnumbered forces.

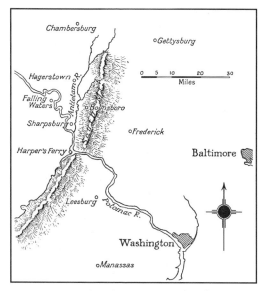

Sharpsburg (Antietam) Battlefield

By late on the fourteenth, Lee knew that Mac was in possession of his plans and was scrambling to throw D. H. Hill's division against the Federal troops at South Mountain. The best Lee could hope for was that his troops would be able to slow down the Union advance long enough for his scattered troops to get reunited. Although the efforts made by the desperate Southerners around South Mountain did manage to slow Mac's advance, the Army of the Potomac successfully advanced through a place known as Fox Gap. This important victory, however, was gained at the expense of the brave Union commander Jesse Reno. As this general was leading the advance guard through Fox Gap, a musket ball was accidentally fired into his side during the fierce fighting. The fatal shot came from the misguided hands of a green Union soldier from the Thirty-fifth Massachusetts. Another friend and classmate of McClellan's was dead.

After the Union breakthrough, Lee ordered his men to pull back toward the nearby town of Sharpsburg. The tiny divisions commanded by Generals Longstreet and D. H. Hill quickly rallied to the call and established a unified defensive position alongside the troops that rode with Lee. The Confederate forces placed themselves in triangular formation behind a small creek called the Antietam, while also taking advantage of the surrounding hills to provide their army with the high ground. Although the defensive position chosen by Lee was advantageous in some respects, it had one major drawback, the swollen Potomac River ran all along his line of retreat. In other words, Lee was virtually trapped and would have to hope that his meager army of 18,000 men could withstand the mighty blows that were surely coming its way.

All that Lee could do was send orders to Stonewall Jackson and A. P. Hill, who were commanding divisions at Harper's Ferry, urging them to send reinforcements to the Sharpsburg and Antietam battlefield. General Lee needed all the troops he could muster and he needed them fast. McClellan was cautiously moving his 85,000 man army toward Sharpsburg and all Lee could do was pray that his relief force arrived in time to save his army from sure destruction.

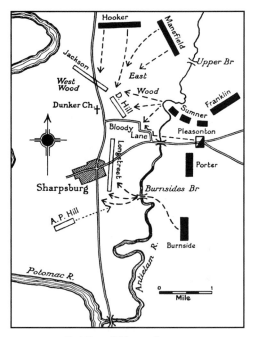

Battle of Sharpsburg

Confederate Generals Longstreet and D. H. Hill had so skillfully placed their troops on the battlefield, that General McClellan decided not to attempt an immediate assault upon the Confederate positions as he arrived on September 15. He would maneuver his army into position during the fifteenth and sixteenth while probing for weaknesses in the Army of Northern Virginia. As events would later prove, the Federal troops would have to pay dearly for Mac's unwillingness to immediately secure the bridges that crossed Antietam

Creek. As usual, General McClellan had no idea that on September 15, he had nearly four times as many soldiers as Lee. If Mac had realized how much of an advantage he had upon his arrival at Sharpsburg, he surely would have sent his forces ahead immediately and pushed the Southern forces into the Potomac. The careful and cautious McClellan was true to his military code or philosophy—he hesitated to attack until he was sure that the lives of his men would not be wasted.

Major General George B. McClellan articulated his view of how military operations should be conducted as he wrote:

> The true course in conducting military operations is to make no movement until the preparations are as complete as circumstances will permit and never to fight a battle without some definite object worth the probable loss; such a course will ever insure the greatest economy of life, time and treasure, as well as the most decisive results.

General McClellan's Headquarters During the Battle of Sharpsburg

It would have been totally out-of-character for George McClellan to throw his forces into a battle without first taking the time to carefully orchestrate his troops. General McClellan waged war by the conservative standards he learned at West Point and by the code of ethics taught by Jesus Christ. He was a true Christian warrior, trying to honorably administer military operations while under the watchful eye of politicians who cared little for such priorities. A whole new philosophy of warfare was beginning to grip the increasingly impatient leaders in the North, and George McClellan's old-fashioned principles were not going to be tolerated much longer. The battle at Antietam was Mac's last opportunity to prove that he had the zeal necessary to prosecute the war with reckless abandon. As we will soon see, the conservative McClellan would discover that caution does not always enable a field commander to reduce casualties and human misery.

On September 15, Stonewall Jackson sent a message to Lee informing him of the fact that his corps had captured Harper's Ferry along with eleven thousand Federal troops. A grateful Lee responded by ordering General Jackson to come immediately to Sharpsburg. Stonewall Jackson set out to rejoin Lee and left his old West Point classmate A. P. Hill in charge of overseeing matters at Harper's Ferry.

General Joe Hooker

General McClellan met with his field commanders on the evening of the sixteenth and gave them their battle orders. The right wing of McClellan's forces under Joe Hooker and Joseph Mansfield would cross the Antietam Creek and engage the enemy's left flank early on the seventeenth. At the same time, the left wing of Mac's army, under the command of Ambrose Burnside would attack the right flank of Lee's forces after crossing a bridge over the Antietam. McClellan planned to outflank the Confederates and eventually send a huge force against the center of Lee's weakened line. The plan was well designed and with bold and unified execution was almost sure to succeed. As the Army of the Potomac made final preparations for battle and bedded down for the night a strange rumbling sound could be heard in the distance.

The noise came from the thousands of weary men who were a part of Thomas Jackson's corps. These desperately needed reinforcements took their place on the left of Lee's line and prepared to meet the advancing Federal troops under Hooker. All through the night fragments of Lee's army, once scattered across the Maryland countryside continued to trickle into the Confederate camps. By morning, Lee's fractured army could boast almost 40,000 men, considerably better than the 18,000 he possessed only two days previous.

General Hood

In addition to sheer numbers, General Lee had the comfort of knowing that most of his key field commanders were in place at Antietam. Jackson, Longstreet, Hood, J. E. B. Stuart, and McLaws were all present and accounted for even if they were a bit weary and saddle sore. The only commander that Lee lacked was the audacious and spirited A. P. Hill, and even this soldier would find a way to arrive at the battlefield at a strategic moment with a division of reinforcements.

As the battle of Antietam began, the roar of cannon could be heard at the breakfast table of nearly every home in the vicinity of

Sharpsburg. Newspaper reports described it as "a continuous roar, like the unbroken roll of a thunderstorm." At day break, McClellan ordered General Hooker to move his entire first corps against the Confederate left. Soon after, thousands of Federal troops were rushing across the cornfields and small hills toward the positions held by Stonewall Jackson's men. A bloody fight quickly ensued as each side attacked each other with massive waves of men who were desperately trying to force each other into retreat. In the early going, Hooker's men were able to push Jackson's divisions to the point of peril but the gaps in the Confederate line were quickly filled by reinforcements supplied by General Hood. As the morning hours passed, the Federal troops under Hooker were repulsed by the stubborn Confederates and forced to regroup. Both sides suffered very heavy casualties.

Union General Mansfield followed up the stalled movement against the Confederate left as he moved forward with his Twelfth Corps. Moments later, thousands of Federal troops were once again engaging the combined forces under Stonewall Jackson and General Hood. The Union commanders hoped to punch a large hole in the Confederate line before Lee could bring in reinforcements as more of his troops continued to arrive on the battlefield from distant locations. Lee ordered the troops under Generals Walker and McLaws to attack the surging Union advance. They hit the Union troops hard and fast as men fell by the thousands. George McClellan ordered the Second corps under veteran Edwin Sumner and the reorganized First corps under Hooker to answer the Confederate counterattack with one of their own.

The battle was now in full fury as brother fought brother on a scale such as was seldom seen during the War Between the States. Most of the fighting was not done from concealed bunkers or fortified positions, it was simply a case of soldiers slaughtering one another in open fields. During the Union counterattack, the fighting became so fierce and confusing that General Joe Hooker was shot through the foot and his fellow commander Mansfield was mortally wounded. As the smoke cleared and the intensity of the fighting finally slackened, the eight thousand Confederates under Jackson could scarcely believe that their positions had held. They had faced an advance of thirty thousand Federal troops and managed to find a way to stop them from turning the left flank of their army.

General McClellan then ordered an offensive against the right center of the Confederate positions at a place known as the sunken road. Lee had concentrated several pieces of artillery along the sides of this ravine-like pathway and the Confederate gunners pounded thousands of Federal troops as they sought to advance along this dirt road. The relentless Union attack continued to press forward in spite of the fact that brave men were being shot down left and right. By the early afternoon, however, Federal artillery positions had managed to position an extensive field battery on the heights above the sunken road. This artillery position opened up upon the Confederate troops with rifled guns that could shoot much better and further than any weapon in Lee's army. In under an hour, these Union guns pounded the Confederate center into submission. Regrettably for the Union cause, this success was not followed up by a renewed assault. McClellan and his generals were satisfied with merely holding their ground at this central point on the battlefield.

General Ambrose Burnside

After a brief lull in the fighting, McClellan ordered General Burnside to move his division against the Confederate right. In fact, Mac had directed Burnside to move forward hours earlier and was forced to reissue orders regarding this assault when it became apparent that no troops had crossed the arched bridges over Antietam Creek by noon. What General McClellan did not realize was that his longtime friend and roommate "Old Burn" had sent an assault team to capture and cross the bridge over Antietam during the morning hours. This first move against the bridge was doomed to failure, however, as the commander was unable to locate the bridge due to poor visibility and strong enemy fire. After the first assault team returned with its embarrassed leader, Burnside sent his trusted friend, Sam Sturgis forward with troops from the Second Maryland and the Sixth New Hampshire. These men found the bridge, but were unable to successfully pass over it due to the fact that the stone bridge and its approaches were entirely exposed to constant fire from the enemy. In spite of repeated assaults, the Federal forces were unable to get any troops over the Antietam alive. General Burnside was in a true dilemma because he knew that he must quickly find a way to make the orders of McClellan work. He had to get men, lots of men across the Antietam.

The main musket and artillery fire from the Confederate right was concentrated upon what became known as "Burnside's bridge." Lee knew that he could not permit a simultaneous assault on his left and right. As a result, the Confederates knew that the longer they

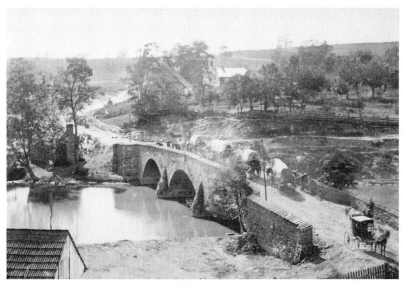

The Stone Bridge Across the Antietam River

could tie up Burnside's division at the bridge over Antietam, the longer General Lee could continue to loan troops to his beleaguered left flank. George McClellan was getting tired of not knowing why the assault on Lee's right flank was delayed. The original plan of General McClellan called for his army to launch a coordinated attack against both sides of the Confederates at Sharpsburg. The problems encountered by Burnside, however, caused the comprehensive plan of George McClellan to quickly degenerate into a series of separate uncoordinated attacks. As long as Lee could keep Mac's army from hammering him at multiple points along his line, he just might be able to avert disaster and at least achieve something of a standoff.

Notwithstanding the good news that Lee received regarding Burnside's bridge, he knew that he would need to bring in at least one more potent weapon to cope with the inevitable Federal advance. One thing was for sure, the Confederate army was not going to keep Burnside's division tied up at a stone bridge indefinitely. At this critical hour, Robert E. Lee sent orders to A. P. Hill who was commanding the Confederate forces at Harper's Ferry. Hill was told to march his famous Light Division seventeen miles to Sharpsburg, as rapidly as possible. If Lee was counting on General Hill to be his "stand in the gap" soldier, he picked the right man.

The reputation of A. P. Hill preceded him into Sharpsburg. Hill was exactly the type of soldier that was needed when an impossible task needed to be done. He was bold, fierce in battle and totally audacious. His red beard, and wavy hair were complemented by the bright red flannel shirt that he often wore in battle. If ever a man was born for battle, it was A. P. Hill. He was, in every respect, the complete opposite of George McClellan. Mac was a cultured military gentleman who prided himself upon the virtues of prudence, caution, and careful organization. Hill was a restless fighter who thought little of protocol or decorum. In A. P. Hill's economy, the field commander was paid to do one thing, win battles and in the process drive his men as hard as the military situation dictated. As a consequence, Hill often brought his men past the point of their natural abilities by his sheer determination. Little wonder why A. P. Hill was regarded as "Lee's Hammer."

It took Hill's division one hour to depart from Harper's Ferry en route to Sharpsburg and glory. All along the hot and dusty trail, General Hill poked, prodded and even threatened his men as he drove them northward. Finding the battlefield at Sharpsburg was no challenge at this stage of events. The constant drone of cannon could be heard from miles away and Hill's men certainly did not need anyone to tell them what that meant. Generals Lee and Hill both hoped that the reinforcements from Harper's Ferry would arrive in time to save the day.

In the early afternoon, Mac wired his wife stating, "We are in the midst of the most terrible battle of the age." McClellan's statement was not far from the truth. The one-day battle was easily the bloodiest of the Civil War and would shock the entire nation.

A mere twenty-five hundred men stood on the Confederate right between Burnside's men and the town of Sharpsburg. Burnside was anxious to push these stubborn soldiers back into Sharpsburg and in the process cut off Lee's only line of retreat across the Potomac. If and when that happened, the Army of Northern Virginia would be finished. More than ever, it seemed clear to Lee that A. P. Hill's division simply had to reach the battlefield in time to halt Burnside's advance toward Sharpsburg. Time, however, was beginning to run out.

By 1:30 in the afternoon, General Burnside ordered Sam Sturgis to lead a fresh assault against the infernal stone bridge. Sturgis sent the Fifty-first New York and the Fifty-first Pennsylvania into battle with directions to storm the bridge with fixed bayonet. Thousands of Federal troops charged bravely over their objective and at last engaged the Confederate right on the other side of Antietam Creek. Sturgis halted his men from advancing further in the direction of Sharpsburg, however, in order to resupply them with fresh ammunition and additional reinforcements. It took General Sturgis almost two hours to prepare his units to advance upon the Confederate right. During this critical period, McClellan sent several messages to

General Burnside ordering him to advance his forces immediately upon the enemy positions. Burnside merely replied to his friend and commander, George McClellan, that he thought that he could hold the bridge area without difficulty.

For the first time in recent memory, McClellan became enraged with the conduct of his old friend, General Burnside. In between puffs of cigar smoke, Mac snorted, "He should be able to do that with five thousand men; if he can do no more I must take the remainder of his troops and use them elsewhere in the field." George McClellan had finally lost patience with his friend due to the fact that Burnside's inability to engage the Confederate right until almost three o'clock in the afternoon had significantly upset Mac's battle plan.

Notwithstanding the shortcomings of Burnside's leadership, and the general lack of progress, things were beginning to look rather hopeful for the Union cause. The Confederate troops on the left had been badly bloodied during the morning hours and were totally exhausted. What remained of Lee's right flank was outnumbered almost five to one by the fresh troops under the command of General Burnside. The only thing standing between the Confederates and disaster were a few thousand men and some well-positioned artillery. Most of the outnumbered Confederates knew that they could not hold back the gigantic tide of Federal infantry that was finally beginning to advance in their direction. Thankfully for Lee, his men were too tired to run away. As one brave Confederate soldier put it, "we stood our ground more from a blind dogged obstinacy than anything else... giving them fire for fire, shot for shot, and death for death." All that Lee's men could hope to do was to slow down the Union attack and pray for Hill's men to arrive.

The ground seemed to shake as the massive tide of Union infantry fought its way up toward the heights around Sharpsburg. The Confederate artillery tore into the Federal ranks, but the Union advance continued to roll on like a mighty locomotive. At about 3:30 in the afternoon, however, General Burnside began to receive reports regarding a strong enemy force that was moving toward the left flank of his advancing division. Great clouds of dust were seen in the direction of Sharpsburg and that could only mean one thing— Hill's men had arrived in the nick of time. The great God of battles had, indeed, answered the prayers of Lee. As Hill's brigades prepared to smash into the exposed Union flank, their rough and ready commander, A. P. Hill, was receiving his orders from a greatly relieved general by the name of Robert E. Lee. The meeting between Lee and Hill was brief and emotional, both men knew what needed to be done. After a few brief instructions, Hill rode off to his unit.

Minutes later, A. P. Hill had his men in battle order and was poised to descend upon the unsuspecting enemy. For some reason, Burnside did not regard the news of the threat to his left flank seriously. That was a big mistake, for by the time that the Federal troops knew what hit them, it would be too late to respond effectively.

As A. P. Hill's division tore into the surging Federal line, its men let out the familiar rebel yell. Suddenly, the great blue giant staggered and hesitated, and as it hesitated, it was lost. The effect of Hill's attack on the left wing of Burnside corps was to roll it up like a scroll. Confederate General James Longstreet witnessed the amazing transformation and testified that Hill's men seemed to spring "from the earth." The once grand and orderly advance of the mighty Burnside corps soon began to dissolve into a mass of confusion and retreat. The sound of cannons, the clash of arms, and whirling swords all blended together with the screams of dying and dejected men.

Shortly before darkness set in, the division under Burnside staggered back to the banks of the Antietam. Both armies were totally exhausted and ready to call it a day—and what a day it had been! As the sun set upon the battlefield, both armies essentially occupied the identical positions that they had enjoyed in the morning with the exception of the fact that the Federal troops would retain control of Burnside's bridge. Twenty three thousand Americans—North and South—were killed during this historic battle, yet the fighting resulted in little more than a gruesome stalemate.

A great deal of the fighting that took place during the battle of Antietam was directed by field commanders like Burnside and A. P. Hill. During much of the day, both Lee and McClellan often found themselves out of control and forced to play the role of spectator. Small but significant mistakes were made by both commanders and their respective subordinates. The real hero of the day's battle was, of course, General A. P. Hill. His magnificent effort to drive his tired division seventeen miles and then lead it into a strategic attack against a numerically superior enemy, was nothing short of amazing. Few field commanders, including George McClellan, would have the gumption to drive their men as hard as A. P. Hill did at Sharpsburg.

After the battle, both armies used the nighttime hours to bury their dead and care for their wounded. The toll in human suffering was staggering as men were desperately trying to care for sick and dying comrades. As casualty reports began to arrive at McClellan's headquarters around midnight, he decided to order his officers to hold their ground the next morning. They were told not to attack or advance unless attacked by the enemy. Mac would only renew his offensive against Lee after his blood-stained army was resupplied and reorganized. As a consequence, the next day both armies stared each other down and fought minor skirmishes.

When General Lee realized that McClellan was not going to immediately follow up his offensive, he decided to move his army across the Potomac to safer ground. As Lee's men moved out under cover of darkness, Mac would reluctantly decide not to aggressively pursue his foe. General McClellan could not bring himself to commit his remaining reserves to the battle against Lee even though his army was still almost twice the size of the Army of Northern Virginia. As a result, George McClellan lost the opportunity of a lifetime.

Many historians have attempted to probe into the probable reasons why General McClellan could never quite bring himself to the point of risking his army's security. It is often noted that Mac was reluctant to wage aggressive warfare because he had a tender heart towards his fighting men. He could not stand to see them suffer. The irony of this observation is that McClellan's great love for his soldiers actually worked against the goals of his army and made it difficult for Mac to fully utilize the potential of his men. In the case of the Battle of Antietam, McClellan knew that his men fought harder during the first day's battle than ever before. He was, in fact, convinced that his men were totally fought out and that it would be unreasonable to push them beyond their apparent limits. All day long at Antietam, Mac witnessed the suffering of his battered troops and he dreaded the thought of prolonging their misery. From one end of the war to the other, the Army of the Potomac never lost as many men as it did at Antietam: not at Gettysburg, not in the Wilderness, not anywhere. General McClellan's capacity for sending his men in to be hurt had simply been exhausted. Unlike General A. P. Hill, Mac did not possess the killer instinct or warrior spirit that would be necessary to order hurting men into a prolonged battle. As a consequence, Mac's army would be spared the challenges of a renewed battle at Antietam but would be required to go on fighting until 1865.

As the sun began to rise on the morning to September 19, George McClellan looked out upon a field that had been abandoned by his enemies. A few hours rest had put the young Napoleon in a more optimistic state of mind. He sat down and wrote his wife stating, "those in whose judgment I rely tell me that I fought the battle splendidly and that it was a masterpiece of art." Later in the afternoon, Mac wired General-in-chief Halleck in Washington stating, "I have the honor to report that Maryland is entirely freed from the presence of the enemy, who have been driven across the Potomac. No fears need now be entertained for the safety of Pennsylvania. I shall at once occupy Harper's Ferry."

In fairness to General McClellan, it should be stressed that the vast majority of his officers felt exactly the same way that he did regarding a renewed offensive against Lee. On September 18th, nearly every field commander in the Army of the Potomac was convinced that their men should not be pressed into battle on the eighteenth. One reason for this perspective was that most Union commanders fully expected the Confederates to renew their attack sometime during the second day of action. It should also be acknowledged that McClellan did order a cavalry unit to pursue Lee on the nineteenth. A brigade under General Fitz John Porter crossed over the Potomac River on September 20, with the approval of General McClellan, and attacked the rear guard of the fleeing enemy. This attack was not well coordinated, however, and a counter attack by A. P. Hill's men drove Porter's troops back into Maryland. Although the pursuit of McClellan's army could not be termed as aggressive, the fact remains that Mac did make some genuine effort to inflict further damage upon the Confederates.

In the days following the Battle of Antietam, the Army of the Potomac was also busy fighting small skirmishes with pockets of Confederate cavalry that were in the vicinity of Sharpsburg and Shepherdstown. During this time frame, George McClellan was busy dealing with his wounded men and processing 6,000 Confederate prisoners that had fallen into his hands.

A close friend of George McClellan, by the name of W. C. Prime, relates a touching story of one lady who happened to meet General McClellan shortly after the Battle of Antietam. This woman, who lived in New York, had seen her brother's name on the list of those soldiers killed at Antietam. She therefore determined to travel to the place of her brother's burial to find his grave. What this woman experienced upon arriving at the battlefield was tenderly recorded by Mr. Prime. He states:

> She found her way to the battlefield, and after a while to the graves where some one told her the approximate location where her brother's regiment were buried. It was a lonesome place above ground then, for the army had moved away. She was searching among the graves for a familiar name on the stakes, when she saw, riding down the road which passed at some distance from the burial place, what she called a lot of soldiers on horseback. When they came abreast of her the leader, who was a little in advance, called a halt, sprang to the ground, and walked across the open

field to her. "What are you looking for, my good woman?" he said. She told him. "What was your brother's regiment?" She answered. "You are only one of thousands who want to know today where their dead are lying here," he said. "I hope you will find your brother's grave. Don't mourn too much for him. He died a soldier's death." Then, turning, he called, "Orderly!" A soldier came. "Stay with this woman and help her find her brother's grave. Report to me this evening." And he went back, remounted, and the company rode on at a gallop. After a while the orderly found the grave, and she knelt there and prayed. Then she asked the soldier: "Who was that gentleman that told you to help me?" "That?" said the orderly. "Why, didn't you know him? That was 'Little Mac.'" "'God bless him!' I said," was the end of her story.

This short story provides a helpful glimpse into the life of George McClellan in terms of his spiritual growth or sanctification in the Christian faith. It reveals the significant progress that Mac had made since the days of his youth, when he struggled almost daily with the sin of pride and self-centeredness. The Lord Jesus Christ was helping George McClellan grow up into true Christian manhood and was enabling him to realize that he must never dwell upon his own problems so deeply that he fails to regard the problems of his neighbor.

As General McClellan renewed his communication with General-in-chief Halleck and Edwin Stanton, he began to notice a distinct lack of praise emanating from the leaders at Washington.

What the frustrated general did not fully comprehend was that his arch enemy, Edwin Stanton, was issuing statements to the media regarding Antietam that were very damaging to Mac's reputation. Stanton, for all practical purposes, controlled the telegraph office at the White House. Not surprisingly, he took full advantage of any opportunity he could find to submit disparaging reports around Washington about McClellan and anyone else who was in his way. As soon as General McClellan became aware of the negative wave of propaganda that was circulating around Washington regarding his actions at Antietam, he knew that he was going to be blamed for the fact that the war and the institution of slavery were not brought to a speedy end. Once again, McClellan would have to battle the enemy in his rear. This time, however, he would not be able to count on the continued support of President Lincoln. The desperate Commander-in-Chief was about to abandon Mac's limited view of the war in favor of the radical cause. Lincoln believed that he was required to save the Union by any means possible, even if it included the suspension of portions of the United States Constitution.

General McClellan wrote his beloved wife the following letters on September 20 and 22, summarizing his predicament and affirming his faith in God's superintending providence.

> Sept. 20, 9:00 P.M., camp near Sharpsburg.— ...I feel that I have done all that can be asked in twice saving the country. If I continue in its service I have at least the right to demand a guarantee that I shall not be interfered with. I know I cannot have that assurance so long as Stanton continues in the position of Secretary of War and Halleck as general-in-chief.... I can retire from the service for sufficient reasons without leaving any stain upon my reputation. I feel now that this last short campaign is a sufficient legacy for our child, so far as honor is concerned.... You should see my soldiers now! You never saw anything like their enthusiasm. It surpasses anything you ever imagined.... My tent is filled quite to overflowing with trophies in the way of captured secesh battle-flags. We have more than have been taken in all battles put together, and all sorts of inscriptions on them....

> Sept. 22, 9:00 A.M.— ...I rode out on the battlefield yesterday. The burial of the dead is by this time completed; and a terrible work it has been, for the slain counted by thousands on each side.... I look upon this campaign as substantially ended, and my present intention is to seize Harper's Ferry and hold it with a strong force; then go to work and reorganize the army and make it ready for another campaign.... I shall not go to Washington, if I can help it, but will try to reorganize the army somewhere near Harper's Ferry or Frederick.... It may be that, now that the government is

pretty well over their scare, they will begin again with their persecutions and throw me overboard again. I don't care if they do. I have the satisfaction of knowing that God has, in His mercy, a second time made me the instrument for saving the nation, and am content with the honor that has fallen to my lot. I have seen enough of public life. No motive of ambition can now retain me in the service. The only thing that can keep me there will be the conviction that my country needs my services and that circumstances make it necessary for me to render them. I am confident that the poison still rankles in the veins of my enemies at Washington, and that so long as they live it will remain there.... I have received no papers containing the news of the last battle, and do not know the effect it has produced on the Northern mind. I trust it has been a good one, and that I am reestablished in the confidence of the best people of the nation.... Everything quiet today; not a shot fired as yet. I am moving troops down to Harper's Ferry, and hope to occupy it tomorrow. Then I will have the Potomac clear....

George McClellan knew that he did not possess the respect and confidence of the politicians in Washington. He was rather sure, however, that he had honored God in his recent service for his country and still held the full support of his officers and men. This assurance provided Mac with the strength he needed to continue on with his mission.

Chapter Ten

The Disposable Patriot

1862–1863

P resident Abraham Lincoln, like most officials at Washington, had hardly said one word to George McClellan since the battle of Antietam. Lincoln's only message to the Young Napoleon simply stated, "Your despatch received. God bless you and all with you! Can't you beat them some more before they get off?"

One reason for the President's lack of communication and congratulation was that he was busy issuing two historic proclamations. On September 22, Lincoln issued the preliminary Emancipation Proclamation and a couple of days later ordered the suspension of the right of *habeas corpus* along with approval of martial law procedures for any citizen charged with discouraging enlistments or engaging in any "disloyal practice." General McClellan, and many other pro-Union

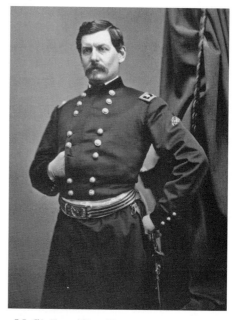

McClellan, The Disposable Patriot

Americans viewed the proclamations issued by Lincoln to be the acts of a despot or traitor. To George McClellan, in particular, these

Presidential orders were destined to change the focus of the war from reunification to social and political revolution.

General McClellan, and several of his top officers, had discussions in late September regarding the recent political pronouncements by Lincoln. One of Mac's closest friends, General Fitz John Porter, actually went so far as to issue statements to the editor of the *New York World*. These statements alleged that the emancipation decree would demoralize the Army of the Potomac and invigorate the Southern cause. Porter accused the abolitionists of prolonging the war by stirring up bitterness in the South thereby making it difficult for the Union army to end the conflict honorably. General Porter stated that the military effort was being fatally "upset by the absurd proclamations of a political coward...." Strong words, indeed, for such a well known and respected military leader.

McClellan had drafted his own letter in opposition to Lincoln's proclamations, but had the sense to consult with high ranking politicians and soldiers before issuing it to the public. Almost everyone who spoke with Mac advised him not to oppose the Lincoln Administration on the issue of slavery and *habeas corpus*. The most compelling argument that Mac received was that it would be "a fatal error" for a military leader of his rank to publicly violate the principle of the subordination of military commanders to civil authority. This point, along with the fact that George McClellan was not opposed to emancipation in principle, caused him to resist the temptation to oppose Lincoln. Mac wisely decided not to publicly oppose the proclamation and determined to quietly continue doing his duty as a soldier.

The reasonable decisions reached by General McClellan in regard to reacting to governmental policies could not have been easy for him to reach. Not only did McClellan have conflicting emotions to deal with, but he also had several military leaders in his army encouraging him to march on Washington for the purpose of taking temporary control over the government. Although Mac never seriously considered the notion of taking over the White House by a military coup, he certainly could have been negatively influenced by this foolish counsel.

First and last, the Emancipation Proclamation was a political document designed to transform the nature of the American conflict in the minds of foreign powers. The act immediately put foreign politicians who were pro-Confederate into the position of being apologists for slavery, whether they liked it or not. In the final analysis, the proclamation meant that Europe was not going to intercede on behalf of the Confederacy and possibly help determine the course of the war. The War Between the States would be fought out to the bitter end by the States themselves.

Prior to the issuing of the Emancipation Proclamation, there had always been the possibility that the war might simply end, with neither side victorious. Many Americans in the opening stages of war, including George McClellan, held out the hope that reunion could somehow be achieved without totally solving the sticky issues of slavery and states' rights. These issues, it was hoped, could be solved gradually and peacefully over a period of time. The proclamation, however, made that impossible. The war had been given a wider and deeper meaning that could not be compromised. Now, all of the central issues that led to the war would have to be settled, not evaded; and settled by violence, violence having been unleashed.

Although many decent Americans living during this era still preferred to argue that the issues of states' rights, a growing central government, and immediate versus gradual emancipation for slaves could be better settled through peaceful means, the argument was no longer relevant. The actions taken by President Lincoln made the war a war to restore the Union and end slavery—two causes in one, the combination carrying its own consequences. Lincoln had desired to avoid a total war where one side or the other was brought to its knees. With the lack of decisive victory on the battlefield, however, Abraham Lincoln reluctantly decided to permit the American Civil War to turn vicious and comprehensive. This new approach to the war required that Lincoln put military commanders into place that were willing to prosecute the war in terms of the radical agenda of subjugating the South. Generals like Sheridan were needed to carry total devastation against military and civilian installations in the Shenandoah Valley. Men like Sherman were required to swing a torch across Georgia and leaders like Grant had to be found who could unmercifully grind the Southern armies into dust. The Confederacy now had to be comprehensively crushed to death by relentless effort. Southern soldiers needed to be extinguished, along with the spirit, resources, and culture that spawned the Confederacy in the first place. From this point forward, it would all be grim and total war, which meant, in part, that McClellan's place in the struggle was all but finished.

The reaction of many in Lincoln's home state of Illinois to the Emancipation Proclamation was less than favorable. It should be remembered that Illinois, Ohio, and Indiana were strongholds of the Copperhead Movement. The Copperheads were Northern people whose sympathies lay, in many respects, with the South.

On January 7, 1863, the Democratic legislature of Illinois issued its statement of opposition to Lincoln's proclamation. It stated:

> Resolved: That the Emancipation Proclamation of the President of the United States is as unwarrantable in military as in civil laws; a gigantic usurpation, at once converting the war professedly commenced by the administration for the vindication of the authority of the Constitution, into the crusade for the sudden, unconditional, and violent liberation of 3,000,000 negro slaves; a result which would not only be a total subversion of the Federal Union but a revolution of the social organization of the Southern states, the immediate and remote, the present and far-reaching consequences of which to both races cannot be contemplated without the most dismal foreboding of horror and dismay. The proclamation invites servile insurrection as an element in this emancipation crusade—a means of warfare, the inhumanity and diabolism of which are without example in civilized warfare, and which we denounce, and which the civilized world will denounce, as an ineffaceable disgrace to the American people.

The true political and cultural ramifications of the Emancipation Proclamation were not lost on George McClellan. Nevertheless, the Young Napoleon also understood that his true calling was as the head of the Army of the Potomac. He was still a soldier with an important job to perform and his men were counting on him to lead them to victory. In this spirit, General McClellan pressed forward with the business of refitting his army for its next mission.

Mac wired General-in-chief Halleck in late September requesting various supplies and equipment for his men. He was particularly interested in receiving a new shipment of horses for his cavalry troops due to the fact that many of his horses had been wounded or were fighting various diseases. General McClellan also informed Halleck and Lincoln that, in his view, "This army is not now in condition to undertake another campaign nor to bring on another battle..." This observation, as one would expect, was interpreted by the officials at Washington as nothing more than an excuse for Mac to waste more time. While the roads were still dry and the weather pleasant, President Lincoln determined to do everything possible to push little Mac into a fresh battle with Lee's army. The President therefore decided to visit the Army of the Potomac and speak directly to its conservative general.

Abraham Lincoln arrived at the Sharpsburg battlefield on October 1 for a four-day visit filled with hospital tours, military reviews, and meetings with leaders like General McClellan. An interesting account of this historic event was recorded by McClellan in his personal memoirs. Mac relates:

> On the first day of October his Excellency the President honored the Army of the Potomac with a visit, and remained several days, during which he went through the different encampments, reviewed the troops, and went over the battle-fields of South Mountain and Antietam. I had the opportunity during this visit to describe to him the operations of the army since the time it left Washington, and gave him my reasons for not following the enemy after he crossed the Potomac.

> He was accompanied by Gen. McClernand, John W. Garrett, the

Secretary of State of Illinois, and others whom I have forgotten. During the visit we had many and long consultations alone. I urged him to follow a conservative course, and supposed from the tenor of his conversation that he would do so. He more than once assured me that he was fully satisfied with my whole course from the beginning; that the only fault he could possibly find was that I was perhaps too prone to be sure that everything was ready before acting, but that my actions were all right when I started. I said to him that I thought a few experiments with those who acted before they were ready would probably convince him that in the end I consumed less time than they did. He told me that he regarded me

Abraham Lincoln Visits General McClellan at Sharpsburg

as the only general in the service capable of organizing and commanding a large army, and that he would stand by me. We parted on the field of South Mountain, whither I had accompanied him. He said there that he did not see how we ever gained that field, and that he was sure that, if I had defended it, Lee could never have carried it.

We spent some time on the battlefield and conversed fully on the state of affairs. He told me that he was entirely satisfied with me and with all that I had done; that he would stand by me against "all comers"; that he wished me to continue my preparations for a new campaign, not to stir an inch until fully ready, and when ready to do what I thought best. He repeated that he was entirely satisfied with me; that I should be let alone; that he would stand by me. I have no doubt that he meant exactly what he said. He parted from me with the utmost cordiality. We never met again on this earth.

He had hardly reached Washington before Cox's division was taken from me and the order of Oct. 6 reached me! A singular commentary on the uncertainty of human affairs!

On the 5th of Oct. the division of Gen. Cox (about 5,000 men) was ordered from my command to Western Virginia.

On the 7th of Oct. I received the following telegram from Gen. Halleck:

"Oct. 6—I am instructed to telegram you as follows: The President directs that you cross the Potomac and give battle to the enemy or drive him south. Your army must move now while the roads are good. If you cross the river between the enemy and Washington, and cover the latter by your operation, you can be reinforced with 30,000 men. If you move up the valley of the Shenandoah not more than 12,000 or 15,000 can be sent to you. The President advises the interior line between Washington and the enemy, but does not order it. He is very desirous that your army move as soon as possible. You will immediately report what line you adopt and when you intend to cross the river; also to what point the reinforcements are to be sent. It is necessary that the plan of your operations be positively determined on before orders are given for building bridges and repairing railroads. I am directed to add that the Secretary of War and the general-in-chief fully concur with the President in these instructions."

After President Lincoln returned to Washington, General McClellan resumed the task of reorganizing and reequipping his troops. A flurry of ill-tempered telegraphs were exchanged between Mac and General-in-chief Halleck concerning the tardiness of supplies that had been ordered through Washington. Lincoln, meanwhile, continued to prod McClellan to advance across the Potomac regardless of his lack of proper supplies. On October 13, President Lincoln reminded Mac of their recent deliberations. "You remember my speaking to you of what I called your overcautiousness? Are you not overcautious when you assume that you cannot do what the enemy is constantly doing? Should you not claim to be at least his equal in prowess, and act upon the claim?" Notwithstanding the attempt by the President to shame the Young Napoleon into action, Mac realized that Lincoln's observations did not put shoes on his soldiers or healthy horses under his cavalry troops. Mac simply ignored the demands of the politicians in Washington who were endeavoring to dictate not only military policy but to presume the right to play field general as well.

While General McClellan was busy hassling with his superiors at Washington, the wily and courageous cavalry General "Jeb" Stuart was once again on the move. Stuart crossed over the Potomac on October 10, with 2,000 cavalry troops and made a series of daring raids in parts of Maryland and Pennsylvania. This action enabled "Jeb" Stuart to ride completely around McClellan's army for the second time, while Federal detachments ran all over western Maryland searching for him. This event demonstrated the glaring problems that existed within Union cavalry circles. The raid by "Jeb" Stuart also served to strengthen the Confederate cavalry as Stuart's men were able to return to their lines with over 1,200 captured horses.

General "Jeb" Stuart

The bickering between Mac and the officials at Washington became more pronounced as the month of October unfolded. This was due to the fact that both parties were incapable of listening to each other properly. Washington bureaucrats were unable to fully appreciate the genuine supply needs of a vast army and Mac was unable to comprehend the fact that the Confederate army was in worse shape than his own and needed to be pressed before Lee could rebuild his forces. The only relief that General McClellan enjoyed from his growing problems came in the form of a two-week visit from his wife, daughter and mother-in-law. Mac had the pleasure of visiting his family on almost a daily basis at a farmhouse near his camp at Sharpsburg.

Five weeks after the Battle of Antietam, General McClellan was finally in the position to telegraph Halleck and inform him of the fact that he had decided "to move upon the line indicated by the President...." Mac sent his family back home and began to move his army of 100,000 men over the Potomac into Virginia. The massive columns of the Army of the Potomac moved south along the eastern side of the Blue Ridge. General McClellan was aiming to force Lee to expose his army to attack while Mac's army moved ever closer to Richmond. Much to the dismay of Abraham Lincoln, however, it took ten days for Mac's army to move thirty-five miles. This pace gave Lee ample time to send a large force under General Longstreet to block McClellan's army from positioning itself between the Army of Northern Virginia and its capital.

One of the main reasons for the slow and deliberate pace of McClellan's advance was that Mac's intelligence officer, Allan Pinkerton, had once again given the Union army inflated estimates of the enemy's strength. Pinkerton reported that Lee's army had something close to 130,000 men, when in fact Lee had less than 70,000 soldiers. This faulty intelligence produced, as usual, an attitude of undue caution in the mind of George McClellan and his corp commanders.

When Abraham Lincoln received the news that the Confederate army had out maneuvered the Army of the Potomac and positioned itself at Culpeper Courthouse ahead of McClellan, the President was determined to fire the Young Napoleon. In all likelihood, however, Lincoln had determined to relieve McClellan from command shortly after his visit to the Antietam battlefield. He was simply looking for a convenient excuse to pull the trigger on his conservative general. On November 5, President Lincoln had the following order given to George McClellan by the hand of Brigadier General Catharinus Buckingham:

> *General Orders, No. 182.*
>
> *War Department,*
> *Adjutant-General's Office*
> *Washington, Nov. 5, 1862*
>
> *By direction of the President of the United States, it is ordered that Maj.-Gen. McClellan be relieved from the command of the Army of the Potomac, and that Maj.-Gen. Burnside take the command of that army.*
>
> *By order of the Secretary of War*
>
> *E.D. Townsend*
>
> *Assist. Adj.-Gen.*

The way in which little Mac, the disposable patriot, reacted to his firing was recorded in his memoirs. McClellan describes his late-night meeting with Generals Buckingham and Burnside:

> I saw that both—especially Buckingham—were watching me most intently while I opened and read the orders. I read the papers with a smile, immediately turned to Burnside, and said: 'Well, Burnside, I turn the command over to you.'

> They soon retired, Burnside having begged me to remain for a few days with the army, and I having consented to do so, though I wished to leave the next morning.

> Before we broke up from the Maryland side of the Potomac I had said to Burnside that, as he was second in rank in the army, I wished him to be as near me as possible on the march, and that he must keep himself informed of the condition of affairs. I took especial pains during the march to have him constantly informed of what I was doing, the positions of the various corps, etc., and he ought to have been able to take the reins in his hands without a day's delay.

> The order depriving me of the command created an immense deal of deep feeling in the army—so much so that many were in favor of my refusing to obey the order, and of marching upon Washington to take possession of the government. My chief purpose in remaining with the army as long as I did after being relieved was to calm this feeling, in which I succeeded.

> I will not attempt to describe my own feelings nor the scenes attending my farewell to the army. They are beyond my powers of description. What words, in truth, could convey to the mind such a scene—thousands of brave men, who under my very eye had changed from raw recruits to veterans of many fields, shedding tears like children in their ranks, as they bade good-by to the general who had just led them to victory after the defeats they had seen under another leader? Could they have foreseen the future their feelings would not have been less intense!

Edwin Stanton enlisted the help of General Buckingham who was a friend of generals McClellan and Burnside, to hand deliver the bad news to Mac because he felt that this would make it harder for McClellan to try to ignore the directions of the President. Stanton was also fearful that General Burnside, who was a very close friend of Mac, would be reluctant to accept command of the Army of the Potomac and needed Buckingham to prod him into the new promotion.

As soon as the news regarding Mac's dismissal reached his soldiers, there was an immediate and intense reaction of universal outrage. More than a few units refused to serve without McClellan in place and some men talked openly of marching on Washington to protest the President's order. This reaction was exactly what Stanton, Halleck, and the President would have expected and they were fearful. It was the main reason why they did not fire McClellan sooner. The politicians in Washington were painfully aware that the Army of the Potomac was deeply committed to its general. After all, Mac literally birthed and nursed this body of fighting men and led them with courage and distinction. In light of the growing morale problem created by the discharge of General McClellan, the officials at Washington were forced to ask Mac if he would be willing to encourage his former troops to loyally follow the new command structure. Not surprisingly, Mac issued a parting statement to his men admonishing them to faithfully follow their new leader.

General McClellan also issued the following farewell to the Army of the Potomac.

> *Headquarters, Army of the Potomac,*
>
> *Camp near Rectortown, Va., Nov. 7, 1862*
>
> *Officers and Soldiers of the Army of the Potomac:*
>
> *An order of the President devolves upon Maj.-Gen. Burnside the command of this army.*
>
> *In parting from you I cannot express the love and gratitude I bear to you. As an army you have grown up under my care. In you I have never found doubt or coldness. The battles you have fought under my*

command will proudly live in our nation's history. The glory you have achieved, our mutual perils and fatigues, the graves of our comrades fallen in battle and by disease, the broken forms of those whom wounds and sickness have disabled—the strongest associations which can exist among men—unite us still by an indissoluble tie. We shall ever be comrades in supporting the Constitution of our country and the nationality of its people.

Geo. B. McClellan
Maj.-Gen. U.S. Army

George McClellan was well aware of the fact that his friend, Ambrose Burnside, was now in a very difficult predicament. Mac wrote his wife telling her, "Poor Burn feels dreadful, almost crazy... I am sorry for him, and he never showed himself a better man or truer friend than now."

As future events would prove, General Burnside had good reason to be reluctant to take over an army of 100,000 men. He knew all along, in fact, that he was not fit to lead the Army of the Potomac. He simply agreed to take command in order to keep the position from falling into the hands of Joe Hooker. The only people in the entire Northern military or political establishment that were desperate enough to believe that Burnside could successfully replace McClellan in the middle of an offensive campaign were Stanton, Halleck, and Lincoln.

General Ambrose Burnside

On Monday, November 10, General Burnside rode alongside his departing friend as they trotted past an assembly of weeping and cheering soldiers that was three miles long. Colonel Charles H. Wainwright wrote in his journal, "Such a sight I shall never see again.... Very many of the men wept like children, while others could be seen gazing after him in mute grief... no one on this day could help pronouncing him a good and great man: great in soul if not in mind."

Later that afternoon, Mac would write his wife to confess that, "I never before had to exercise so much self-control. The scenes of today repay me for all that I have endured."

General McClellan and his staff rode to the train station at Warrenton Junction and boarded a special train bound for Washington. On November 11, the train began to speed away from the outposts of the grand Army of the Potomac, an army that would never again see the likes of George McClellan.

Men like Edwin Stanton and General Halleck were not the only ones glad to see McClellan go. Confederate leaders were also happy to see that George McClellan was taken out of action. Southern leader, Henry Kyd Douglas, summed up the feelings of many military men in the Confederacy as he stated, "We seemed to understand his limitations and defects of military character, and yet we were invariably relieved when he was relieved, for we unquestionably always believed him to be a stronger and more dangerous man than anyone who might be his successor." The feeling of the average Confederate foot soldier regarding Mac's dismissal was somewhat different, and yet no less respectful. One Confederate soldier was quoted as saying, "We liked him because he made war like a gentleman: and we loved him for the enemies he had made!"

The reaction by General Robert E. Lee to McClellan's dismissal was also quite interesting. Lee stated that he was concerned that if the Union army kept making changes in command, they might find someone whom he didn't understand. Some historians have chosen to interpret this comment by Lee as a clear indication that he did not respect the abilities of George McClellan. This interpretation, however, does not seem to hold water in light of the remarks that Lee made at a later date to a relative. This relative asked General Lee, "Who, in your opinion, was the ablest Northern general of the war?" "McClellan, by all odds," replied Lee.

It seems rather obvious by the previous quotes, that Robert E. Lee did respect the abilities of George McClellan. He simply believed that although Mac was a very competent foe, his strategies on the field of battle were not beyond his ability to comprehend. Lee's opinion of McClellan was simply that he did not possess a military mind that was superior to his own. When Lee's opinion of Mac is viewed in this light, it causes students of history to plainly recognize what they already knew; that George McClellan was not the equal of Robert E. Lee. It should almost go without saying, however, that the fact of Lee's superiority as a commander does not give anyone the right to diminish the reputation or accomplishments of George McClellan. Few military men in all of history have attained to the level of Lee.

The officials at Washington stationed George McClellan at a post near Trenton, New Jersey, which was close to where his family lived, so he could begin to work on his military reports. Mac still held out the faint hope at this time that he might be given a new command in the West. As the months passed, however, it became clear to all concerned that McClellan would never receive another command.

As Mac began to work on his reports, and partake of the joys of renewed contact with his wife and daughter, General Burnside was moving the Army of the Potomac in a new direction. Burnside decided to discard Mac's plan of campaign in favor of a bold move against the Confederate stronghold at Fredericksburg. The new commander received the applause of the officials at Washington for his aggressive plan and a promise from General Halleck to supply a new bridgehead over the Rappahannock River so his troops could overtake Fredericksburg before it could be fortified by Lee.

Adversely for the Army of the Potomac and General Burnside, the bridges that were supposed to be built over the Rappahannock were only put in place after the Confederates were well positioned

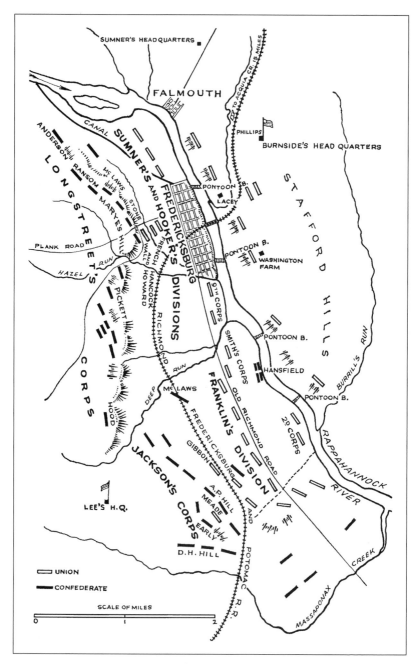

Battle of Fredericksburg

en masse on the heights above Fredericksburg. Although Burnside was not blamed for the delay involved in erecting the needed bridges, he was nevertheless goaded by the authorities at Washington to push forward with his winter campaign against Lee's army.

Ambrose Burnside was so concerned about the dangers confronting his men outside of Fredericksburg, that he traveled to Washington for a few days to directly appeal to his superiors for permission to go into winter quarters. General Burnside explained that his move against Fredericksburg was designed to be a quick strike against Lee before he could place a united force on the high ground around this region. Now that Lee had, once again, foreseen their intentions and taken advantage of the delays of the Union army, Burnside believed that his plan was unworkable.

Notwithstanding the attempted appeal by General Burnside, he was ordered to lead an all out attack upon Lee's army. As soon as the needed bridge was in place, the leery Union commander, Ambrose Burnside, directed his men to storm the Confederate positions south of the river by way of a frontal assault. The result was the slaughter known to history as the Battle of Fredericksburg. Thousands of Federal soldiers lay dead and frozen on the heights south of Fredericksburg, standing as a grim monument to the impatience of the politicians at Washington.

A few weeks later, General Burnside tried to rebound from the loss of Fredericksburg by endeavoring to move his army across the Rappahannock several miles upstream. In this campaign, famous as the "Mud March," the whole army became hopelessly mired, and the campaign had to be abruptly abandoned. Lincoln's wish to have Burnside undertake a midwinter campaign on Virginia soil was thus realized. What McClellan refused to do, General Burnside was willing to try. Five days after Ambrose Burnside was forced to give up his disastrous offensive, President Lincoln dismissed him from command and appointed General Joe Hooker to take his place.

If this sad turn of events would have befallen someone other than General Burnside, George McClellan would surely have been tempted to find the whole affair rather humorous. In reality, however, Mac was just as dismayed as anyone else in the North. After all, many of his closest friends were caught up in the slaughter and embarrassment of the last two campaigns undertaken by the Army of the Potomac.

Not all of the problems that faced the Army of the Potomac, immediately before and after Fredericksburg, can be blamed on the officials at Washington. As previously stated, General Burnside was simply not capable of handling a large army. During his short tenure as the head of McClellan's old army, morale dropped to an all-time low. For one thing, General Burnside rarely spent time personally reviewing and interacting with his troops. He also neglected to ensure that his men received proper food and medical treatment. Those oversights, as well as others, caused the Army of the Potomac to quickly degenerate into a fractured mob instead of a well-organized fighting machine. At one point after the battle of Fredericksburg, it was reported that over two hundred men were deserting the army's ranks on a daily basis! Not surprisingly, many army officers at this time began to lobby for the reinstatement of George McClellan. Brigadier General G. K. Warren of the 5th corps stated, "We must have McClellan back with unlimited and unfettered powers, his name is a tower of strength to everyone here." These appeals, however, would not be enough to force the leaders at Washington to swallow their pride and reinstate Mac.

As the War Between the States continued to grind on the Army of the Potomac would still be required to endure its share of hard times. Their new leader, Joe Hooker would also have to eventually learn the same lesson as his predecessor about how difficult it is to run an army without the consistent cooperation of the officials at Washington.

During early May 1863, the Army of the Potomac moved in great strength against Lee's forces who were positioned near the area known as Chancellorsville. General Hooker soon found himself in the same position as many Union generals before him; he was being treated to an expensive lesson in military tactics compliments of the distinguished Southern generals Lee and Jackson. The battle of

Chancellorsville resulted in yet another tremendous defeat for the Army of the Potomac and General Hooker. The only event in the whole battle that worked to the advantage of the Union army was that the renowned Confederate General Stonewall Jackson was seriously wounded by friendly fire. Ten days after the battle, Jackson died of pneumonia in his weakened condition. Lee had lost his most important general.

General Hooker

The stunning news of Thomas Jackson's death did little to comfort Hooker and his army. The defeat that the Army of the Potomac suffered would keep them on the defensive for several weeks. Lincoln and most of the military leadership in Washington must have been asking themselves, was the situation we had with General McClellan ever this bad?

General Hooker went through the now familiar and expensive routine of reorganizing and reequipping the Army of the Potomac. Meanwhile, on June 3, Lee moved a large body of men into Pennsylvania hoping to catch Hooker in yet another trap. As General Hooker prepared to confront Lee, he sent a telegram off to Washington requesting permission to obtain an additional 10,000 troops from the area around Harper's Ferry. As Hooker began to receive resistance from Washington, he decided to submit his resignation to Lincoln on the heels of his request for more reinforcements. This move was calculated to let the President know that he was ready to resign if he did not get the troops he needed.

Much to the surprise of many Northern military leaders, Lincoln decided to go against his own principle of not swapping horses in midstream. The President relieved Hooker of his command without the slightest hesitation. General George Meade was immediately placed in command of the Army of the Potomac and ordered to put his troops into action against Lee in Pennsylvania.

Much to the displeasure of many soldiers within the Army of the Potomac, President Lincoln had fired three of their

General George Meade

commanders within a span of eight months. The recent appointment of General Meade was naturally received with a certain amount of skepticism by many Union soldiers. In spite of the morale busting actions of President Lincoln, however, the soldiers of the Army of the Potomac managed to keep themselves battle ready. As it turned out, it was a good thing that they did. In less than a month, these brave and bewildered soldiers would finally manage to gain a decisive victory against Lee's army at a place called Gettysburg.

The Union victories at Gettysburg, as well as at Vicksburg, Mississippi, in early July 1863, were truly a turning point in the War Between the States. The Southern forces were finally beginning to sustain the loss of valuable human and material resources at a rate that they could no longer endure. It was the beginning of the end for the Southern struggle for independence. No longer would Lee have the ability to launch a major offensive in the Northern states.

After the events at Gettysburg, Lincoln decided to keep his hands off the leadership of the Army of the Potomac. In fact, General

George Meade remained at the head of this army until the end of the war.

As for George McClellan, he continued to keep busy during 1863 with military reports and with helping the state militia in New York to prepare a volunteer force to help repel the Confederate invasion of Pennsylvania. Mac moved his family's residence to the city of New York in early 1863. While in New York, George McClellan frequently found himself in the public eye where his presence inevitably drew a large crowd. As always, his cheerful and winning personality were the keys to his success. George McClellan was careful, however, not to permit his political differences with the Lincoln administration to discourage the people of the North from supporting the Union soldiers in the field.

In late 1863, many politically active Americans in the North began to speculate as to whether McClellan was, in fact, beginning to groom himself for a run at the White House. After all, the next election season was just around the corner. Mac wrote an interesting letter to his mother in December, 1863 indicating that he would

The New York State Militia Prepares for Battle

not aggressively seek the office of President. He did, however, make it clear that he would wait upon the leading of God's Providence to show him whether it was his calling to seek the Democratic nomination for President. George stated, "I shall do nothing to get it and trust that Providence will decide the matter as is best for the country." As usual, Mac would continue to be open to ways in which he could perform his God-given duties to his countrymen.

Chapter Eleven

Politics and Peace

1863–1865

After General McClellan had returned from his organizational duties with the New York militia during May and June 1863, he decided to move his family out of their 31st Street home in New York City to a rental house on Orange Mountain in New Jersey.

Mac was growing tired of the constant stress that comes with being a public figure in a major city. He also desired to move to a more quiet place in the country for the sake of his wife and young daughter. Many of the major cities in the North, including New York, experienced brief periods of social unrest during 1863. Large scale riots erupted over everything from compulsory military drafts to slavery issues during this turbulent period. This atmosphere was not ideal for a young couple with small children.

General McClellan submitted his final 756 page military report to the War Department on August 4, 1863. This report summarized, howbeit in great detail, his experiences while at the head of the Army of the Potomac. Mac also requested permission from Adjutant General Lorenzo Thomas to publish this report through the government printing office.

True to form, the enemies of George McClellan sought to block the printing of this report for they knew that it would be critical of them. Edwin Stanton and General Halleck were unwilling to permit the report to be printed unless a special appropriation was passed by Congress to fund the printing process. After weeks of delay and political maneuvering, a resolution was finally passed in the House of Representatives calling for McClellan's report to be published. The report appeared in book form during the month of February 1864 and would eventually become the nucleus of another book published after Mac's death entitled *McClellan's Own Story*.

Prior to the Pennsylvania gubernatorial election in mid-October 1863, Mac was approached by his old friends, Samuel S. Cox and Samuel Barlow. These gentleman had been privately encouraging George McClellan for months to throw his hat into the political arena and to run for high office. Mac had already turned down an offer to run on the Democratic ticket for the position of Governor of Ohio. Now McClellan's politically active friends wanted him to publicly endorse the Democratic candidate for Governor in Pennsylvania, Judge George W. Woodward.

Cox and Barlow were convinced that the conservative Democratic candidate for governor would be swept into office if George McClellan came out strongly and publicly for him. On election day, Mac submitted a letter to the Philadelphia Press openly supporting Judge Woodward for governor. McClellan stated that he had met the candidate recently and that he was convinced that he had a correct view of the war and the U.S. Constitution. Mac emphasized the fact that Judge Woodward desired the North to fight according to "the principles of humanity and civilization, working no injury to the private rights and property," and that as a conservative Democrat, he believed that the "sole great objects of this war are the restoration of the unity of the nation, the preservation of the Constitution, and the supremacy of the laws of the country."

Although Woodward lost the election in Pennsylvania, the letter by McClellan had caused quite a number of Americans in the eastern states to sit up and take notice. This action by George McClellan was considered by many to be Mac's first official entry in mainstream political activity. Almost immediately, groups within the Democratic Party began to lobby for McClellan to be listed as the next Presidential candidate for their Party. At this point, however, George McClellan was not quite in the mood to take the political desires of a small number of his countrymen too seriously.

The real priority for Mac during the winter of 1863-64, was to find a way to resign his commission as major-general while at the same time feed his family. The very satisfactory salary of $6,000 per year, for the rank of major-general, was hard to duplicate in the civilian world. On one occasion, George McClellan came close to receiving a position as president of the New Jersey Railroad, but the offer fell through at the last minute.

General McClellan did manage to supplement his income slightly during the early portion of 1864 by writing a series of articles for a new weekly journal called *The Round Table*. These articles covered various military themes such as battlefield communications, military ordinance, a comparison of the armies from Europe and the United States, as well as two articles that were designed to critique the upcoming Union campaigns in the spring. During the latter two articles, McClellan continued to express the view that Richmond must be attacked from the line on the Peninsula that runs along the James River. He also asserted his common opinion that the government's overall policy toward the Southern states must "be in accordance with the enlightened maxims of the New Testament, not with the bloody and barbarous code of the nations of old time, who fought solely to destroy and enslave."

During the election year of 1864, George McClellan's financial holdings took an upward turn, thanks to some wise stock investments that were made on Mac's behalf by longtime friend, William Aspinwall. The railroad stock purchased for George McClellan had increased in value over a twelve month period to the sum of $20,000. As events would later prove, this sum of money would come in very handy.

George and Ellen McClellan decided to stay close to their home at Orange Mountain during much of 1864 for the purpose of establishing something of a normal family life. The war had obviously done a great deal to disrupt their marriage and family routine. Now this couple wished to regroup their family circle and resume the habits consistent with a Christian household including the custom of morning and evening prayers. As the growing pressures of political activity began to descend upon the McClellan household, however, it would be increasingly difficult for them to maintain a tranquil home life.

The Democratic Party was in serious need of finding a candidate that could reunify their fractured ranks. Stephen Douglas, who passed away in 1861, was the last politician that could command the respect of Democratic leaders on a national level. Even Douglas, however, could not keep the Democratic Party from breaking up during the 1860 election, and therefore, the priority of party unity was of paramount importance.

The leaders of the Democratic Party sincerely believed that George McClellan was the only national figure who could unite their followers and give them a victory over the Republican President. At this point in history, the Democratic Party was split between conservatives who supported the war effort for the purpose of restoring the Union alone, and the so-called "peace" Democrats who wanted the war to end regardless of whether the South was restored to the Union. McClellan had always been in the conservative wing of the party. Nevertheless, he was also widely respected by those who were active in the "peace" wing of the Democratic Party.

The question of running for President during the middle of a bloody civil war was not easy for George McClellan to sort out. Mac knew full well that his enemies in the press and the Lincoln Administration would not hesitate to drag his reputation through the mud if he actively showed political ambitions. Indeed, McClellan also understood that even if he was elected, his problems with the radical Republicans in Congress would be nothing short of horrendous. For this reason, Mac was very slow to commit to the possibility of accepting the Democratic nomination for President.

Shortly after George McClellan's military report began to circulate around Washington in late February, politicians on both sides began to pick it apart for the purpose of glorifying or vilifying the would-be politician known affectionately as the Young Napoleon. The newspapers were all too happy to print the latest wild accusations against General McClellan, including a story that accused Mac of meeting with Lee after the Battle of Antietam to make a secret peace deal in exchange for letting the Confederates quietly retreat. Conservative newspapers were willing to permit McClellan to publish his rebuttal to these fanciful accusations but his articles were often written-off by his enemies as political posturing.

Like it or not, George McClellan realized that he was the leading candidate for the Democratic nomination for President and that the national convention for the Democrats was only a few months away. Although the war against the South was going moderately well, many Americans in the North were weary of the struggle. A growing number of conservative Republicans in the North were beginning to show some interest in the moderate views being exposed by George McClellan. This fact had the radical and conservative leaders in the Republican party very worried. They knew very well that their candidate for the 1864 election, Abraham Lincoln, was beginning to lose his popularity. They also knew that if they sat by and permitted McClellan to gain more political momentum, he might very well become the next President of the United States.

Much to the dismay of the Republican politicians at Washington, General McClellan was invited to West Point on June 15 to give a speech dedicating a monument to those Union soldiers who had died in battle. Thousands of patriotic Americans made the effort to travel to West Point so they could hear George McClellan speak. The spectators who witnessed the event did not go home disappointed.

General McClellan rode to the monument site in a military carriage with Brigadier General Robert Anderson of Fort Sumter fame, amidst the cheers and salutes of the enthusiastic crowd at West Point. The carriage stopped in front of the speakers stand as Mac made his way up to the flower strewn platform. The academy band then played "Hail Columbia" and the benedictions soon followed. A short time later, General Robert Anderson moved to the podium and began to introduce the keynote speaker, George McClellan.

Anderson stated, "Fellow-citizens, members of the corps of cadets, and brother soldiers, I have the pleasure of going through the form of introducing to you one who is better known to you than I who introduced him."

McClellan was met with three long and prolonged cheers as he slowly made his way to the podium. From his opening remarks, to the last sentence of his oration, the clear and calm voice of General McClellan could be heard across the northern plain of the academy grounds. He began,

> God knows, that David's love for Jonathan was no more deep than mine for the tried friends of many long and eventful years, whose names are to be recorded upon the structure that is to rise upon this spot.... Such an occasion as this should call forth the deepest and noblest emotions of our nature—pride, sorrow, and prayer; pride that our country has possessed such sons; sorrow that she has lost them; prayer that she may have others like them.

During Mac's speech, which was deliberately non-political in tone, he made a point of blaming the war upon extremist factions in both the North and South. McClellan said that such people were those "for whom sectional and personal prejudices and interests outweighed all considerations for the general good." He also emphasized that the men who fought and died during the war did so for the sake of the Union and the beloved Constitution of the United States.

The address by George McClellan at West Point was widely copied and would eventually be presented at the Democratic National Convention as a portion of the so-called "McClellan Platform." As the influence of McClellan began to spread across the country, men such as Edwin Stanton took every opportunity that was available to harass anyone who befriended Mac.

It was well known that Secretary Stanton made life difficult for members of McClellan's staff as they sought out new military assignments. He also personally took it upon himself to block an effort within the Army of the Potomac to raise money for a presentation sword to honor their army's first commander. As despicable and petty as these actions were, however, the most outstanding example of the wicked schemes of Edwin Stanton was when he dismissed the three members of the West Point administrative staff who were responsible for inviting Mac to speak at their academy. In the long and sordid history of Washington politics, few men have been able to sink to the depths of depravity reached by Edwin Stanton.

While George McClellan was quietly enduring the preposterous political antics of Secretary Stanton, other voices from Washington were privately urging him on in yet another direction. A respected advisor to President Lincoln by the name of Francis P. Blair met with McClellan on July 21 in New York to discuss the possibility of Mac's accepting a new command in exchange for his pledge to abandon the Presidential race. The brief meeting at the Astor House did not produce any concrete results, however, as George McClellan was not willing to compromise his principles by bargaining with the White House for a command.

In spite of the limited results of the above mentioned conference, President Lincoln continued to contemplate the possibility of reinstating General McClellan to a new command. Abraham Lincoln met with his favorite general and military advisor Ulysses S. Grant at Fort Monroe on July 31 and, among other things, discussed the advisability of placing Mac back in action. U.S. Grant made no secret of the fact that he wanted to find some place for McClellan to serve the army. Notwithstanding the positive assertions of General Grant, Lincoln was not interested in having to chase after McClellan in the interest of giving him a new command. As a consequence, nothing ultimately came of this issue and it was soon forgotten.

It is interesting to note the perspective that General Grant had regarding the usefulness of George McClellan. Why, it should be asked, would a man like Grant be favorably impressed with the abilities of George McClellan when so many leaders in Washington had long-since written him off?

It certainly was not because Mac had befriended Grant in any particular way prior to or during the War Between the States. In fact, the few times that these men worked together before the war they usually had plenty of friction. The fact that Ulysses S. Grant did not possess warm personal feelings for Mac did not stop him from acknowledging his remarkable abilities as a professional and experienced soldier. In other words, Grant could afford to take a truly objective and balanced view of General McClellan because he did not have a political agenda to color his perspectives. The leaders at Washington could not honestly make the same claim.

General Grant's view of George McClellan remained the same, even years after the civil war ended. During a frequently quoted interview in 1877, Ulysses S. Grant stated:

> McClellan is to me one of the mysteries of the war. As a young man he was always a mystery. He had the way of inspiring you with the idea of immense capacity, if he would only have a chance…. I have never studied his campaigns enough to make up my mind as to his military skill, but all my impressions are in his favor… the test which was applied to him would be terrible to any man being made a major-general at the beginning of the war. It has always seemed to me that the critics of McClellan do not consider this vast and cruel responsibility—the war, a new thing to all of us, the army new, everything to do from the outset, with a restless people and Congress. McClellan was a young man when this devolved upon him, and if he did not succeed, it was because the conditions of success were so trying. If McClellan had gone into the war as Sherman, Thomas, or Meade, and had fought his way along and up, I have no reason to suppose that he would not have won as high a distinction as any of us.

The War Between the States continued to destroy the lives of thousands of Americans during 1864. The Federal army alone had lost almost 90,000 men between the months of January and August. As a consequence, more and more voices from mainstream groups in the North began to assert the opinion that the war needed to end; even if it meant compromising some of the goals established by the Lincoln administration. A growing number of Northerners, especially in the Democratic Party, were being split into two distinctly different camps. One faction wanted peace first and last—peace at any price, while the other demanded Union first and peace as soon as possible.

It was the desire of many conservative Northerners, like George McClellan, to reconcile the peace wing of the Democratic Party with its more conservative mainstream brethren. Faithful Democrats like McClellan were hopeful that a workable platform could be hammered out during their National Convention scheduled for August 31. Candidate McClellan, however, made it clear that he would not accept the nomination if it meant having to compromise with the peace wing of the party. As events would soon prove, the naive notion that Mac could simply sit back and demand that his political principles be adapted by the delegates at the Convention was wishful thinking. George McClellan, due largely to his inexperience, made the mistake of assuming that his campaign managers could positively influence the platform to the same degree as if he himself was personally involved. McClellan's decision to stay away from the Convention debates and to refrain from the nasty process of political arm twisting cost him dearly.

When the disastrous Democratic Convention finally opened for business, it was all too clear to the McClellan supporters that the conservative direction of the platform was going to be aggressively challenged by the peace Democrats. A "war-failure" resolution was proposed by peace wing leader, Clement Vallandigham as the second plank of the party platform. This resolution, in effect, called for peace at any price and an armistice prior to the point of a political settlement between the states.

The conservatives on the platform subcommittee, who were in McClellan's camp, tried to put in a substitute plank that would make reunion the only pre-condition for peace negotiations, but this initiative fell short of votes in committee. The committee members from the western states were particularly zealous for peace as they did everything in their power to undermine the influence of the conservatives. In the final analysis, the final compromise platform that was drawn up at the Convention clearly favored the peace-wing of the party. Worse yet, the convention delegates were able to nominate George H. Pendleton to the vice-presidential post on the Democratic ticket.

On the heels of adapting a peace platform and a peace wing leader for vice-president, the Chicago convention proceeded to unanimously nominate George McClellan as their Presidential candidate. This move was obviously made in an effort to balance the overall Democratic ticket. What it really did, however, was to all but destroy Mac's opportunity of winning the Presidency. No sooner had the Convention ended, when the Democrats of 1864, including George McClellan, were labeled as the party of treason and disloyalty.

The supporters of McClellan naturally sought to down-play the significance of the party platform and to paint things in the best light possible. As a consequence, Mac was persuaded against his better judgment to accept the nomination. He gave a brief acceptance speech to a small group of supporters who came to congratulate him at his home near Orange Mountain. The next week, he then began to work diligently on constructing his formal acceptance letter. After sixth drafts and numerous revisions, Mac finally believed that he had put together a document that would go a long way toward correcting his party's flawed platform.

This slogan summarized the conservative Democratic platform.

To be sure, the position paper and acceptance letter issued by George McClellan was well constructed and clever. It almost succeeded, in fact, in papering over the deep cracks that existed within the Democratic Party of 1864. Almost is the key word, for Mac was placed in the dilemma of having to alienate either the peace Democrats or the thousands of soldiers who were still fighting for the cause of the Union.

George McClellan chose to alienate the peace Democrats and ran his Presidential race on the theme of "Re-union and Peace with honor." As it turned out, Mac could not afford to alienate any major faction of his supporters and would never be able to overcome to mixed messages that people perceived when they compared his positions to his party's platform. Eventually, as the election drew close at hand, Mac's supporters in the military ranks would also leave him in large numbers. This loss of support from the common soldier was due in part to the fact that significant military victories were achieved during September and October of 1864. In addition, the newspapers had been partially successful in convincing military personnel that George McClellan's loyalty to the war effort was no longer genuine.

Unlike the presidential races of the modern age, where candidates routinely fly all around the country, it was not unusual for a candidate in the 1860s to spend little time traveling across country. This was certainly true for candidates like Lincoln and McClellan, who chose to place themselves in virtual seclusion during much of the campaign. Mac ran, by most anyone's standards, a very low-key campaign. He handled most of the heavy correspondence himself with the help of only one secretary. George McClellan made only two public appearances during the closing weeks of the presidential race. He attended a party rally in Newark in September and a huge torch light parade in New York just days before the election.

In early November, General George McClellan wrote to the adjutant general to resign his military commission for the second and final time. Mac felt that it was appropriate for him to take this step before the election results were in. He knew that his hopes of receiving a command from Lincoln were now gone and he also realized that if he were elected as the next commander-in-chief, he would no longer need a promotion.

The election results were not surprising to George McClellan. He had been prepared for defeat ever since the Chicago Platform was circulated, and now it was official. Mac could solace himself in the fact that he did manage to garner over forty-five percent of the popular vote—almost two million votes in all. Not bad for someone who was running on a shoe-string budget against a powerful Washington political machine! If Mac had any reason for dismay, it may have been on account of the fact that Lincoln received a larger share of the soldiers vote. Some historians have sought to attribute McClellan's poor showing in the military vote to out-and-out fraud. Although these allegations may very well have some merit, it is doubtful that the extent of the fraud would have changed the actual election results significantly.

In reflecting upon the outcome of the election to his friend and political ally Manton Marble, George McClellan wrote, "As I look back upon it, it seems to me a subject replete with dignity—a struggle of honor, patriotism, and truth against deceit, selfishness, and fanaticism, and I think that we have well played our parts. The mistakes made were not of our making and before the curtain falls ... I trust that we will see that these apparent mistakes were a part of the grand plan of the Almighty, who designed that the cup should be drained even to the bitter dregs, that the people might be worthy of being saved."

Mac would later admit to his mother that his brief brush with politics was no less exhausting and frustrating than his experience in the military. "I can imagine no combination of circumstances that will draw me into public life again," said the recently defeated candidate. Mac longed for the quieter life of a simple businessman and with it the solid joys of an uninterrupted domestic life.

As George McClellan began to adjust to life out of the spotlight, he celebrated his thirty-ninth birthday. The former general-in-chief of the Union army must have had a good laugh at this point in his earthly sojourn. Mac's life thus far had been anything but ordinary. He had graduated from West Point as a mere lad and tasted of combat in Mexico. He had blazed a trial through the old West and visited with the kings and royalty of Europe. In his spare time, Mac was a gifted writer and successful inventor. Otherwise, he spent his time commanding all of the Northern armies and literally shaping the Army of the Potomac. As if that was not enough, he decided to take a run at the White House and very nearly won the office of President. All this, before the age of thirty-nine! As George McClellan contemplated his life at so-called middle age, he must have wondered, what on earth could the Lord have left for me to do?

As it would happen, the answer to the question of "What next?" did not become a settled issue for some time to come. Mac had sought a position with the New Jersey Morris and Essex Railroad in late 1864 but the board of directors declined to offer him a position. McClellan's friend, Abram Hewitt, gently explained that the board's decision was based upon a concern that McClellan's political baggage would endanger the railroads relationship with the government. Not surprisingly, Mac interpreted this action as a denial of his right to work and support his family.

This experience so demoralized George McClellan that he reasoned that he had little incentive to stay in a country where such a thing could happen. "I suppose I must make up my mind now to shake the dust off my shoes and go elsewhere—so be it," said Mac to his faithful friend, Samuel Barlow.

Thanks to the successful investments of by-gone years, George McClellan would be able to live quite comfortably off of his savings for a long time. On January 25, 1865, Mac placed himself and his family on a ship headed for England. The McClellans eventually traveled through most of Europe. It was a type of self-imposed exile, American style.

The reception that Mac and his family received in Europe was warm and enthusiastic. Many English citizens regarded McClellan as *the* American general and quite a few had read lengthy excerpts from his military articles and reports. In short, Mac was considered to be a very interesting and glamorous celebrity in the eyes of many people throughout England, and indeed, all of Europe. McClellan wrote his friend, Samuel Barlow from Rome stating:

> I hear no slanders—all treat me as a gentleman, [and] seem disposed to exaggerate very much the importance of my part in the war.... Here we are the equals of the best—at home there is always the wretched feeling of partisan to be encountered. I should be

glad to be able to remain abroad until the expiration of Uncle Abraham's term of service—if gold keeps down, [and] quicksilver up, I may be able to do it. [On the other hand, were I home] there would probably be nothing for me to do but to go into exile in Nevada or Utah for some years....

Mac decided to spend a total of three and a half years touring Europe with his family. During this time, George McClellan spent little time with formal business ventures. He did, however, spend considerable time following the final campaigns of the War Between the States. Mac noted with intense interest the reports concerning Richmond's fall and Lee's surrender at Appomattox Courthouse.

When Mac heard the news regarding Lincoln's assassination, he wrote a friend to tell him that the report struck him with "unmingled horror and regret. How strange it is that the military death of the rebellion should have been followed with such tragic quickness by the atrocious murder of Mr. Lincoln! Now I cannot but forget all that had been unpleasant between us, [and] remember only the brighter parts of our intercourse."

One of the few public statements attributed to George McClellan regarding the war's ending, was recorded during a talk that Mac gave to a group of Americans in Switzerland who were celebrating the Fourth of July. Mac told his assembled countrymen that he sincerely

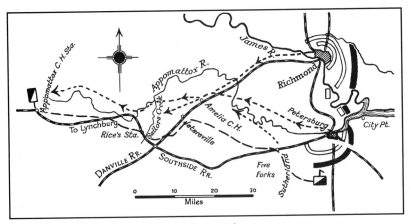

Lee Surrenders at Appomattox

hoped that the new peace would usher in a new era of unity in the United States. George McClellan stated, in part,

> I trust... that, since we have completely vindicated our national strength and military honor by the entire defeat [and] ruin of our late enemies, our people will pursue a magnanimous and merciful course towards a fallen foe—one that will tend to soften the bitter feelings inevitably caused by a long [and] earnest war....

Grand Review in Washington at War's End

It would take almost two years of additional time for George McClellan to finally get homesick enough to return to his homeland. Until then, he would enjoy the peace and quiet of a foreign land where almost everyone was his friend.

Chapter Twelve

Life Goes On

1865–1885

The McClellan family spent most of the spring of 1865 touring through the historical wonders of Rome. Mac wrote his old army buddy, William Franklin stating, "I feel fully compensated for all the miseries of the last few years by the privilege of seeing Rome. This is certainly the most interesting place in the world...."

As the summer season began, George McClellan moved his family to a small hotel on Lake Geneva in Switzerland. While in the city of Geneva, Mac enjoyed visiting the home of the late Reformer and Christian theologian, John Calvin (1509–1564). The writings of Calvin had been very beneficial to the spiritual life of George McClellan and his family. Mac also enjoyed taking boat rides leisurely around Lake Geneva and hiking in the nearby mountains. During this peaceful time, McClellan also began to work on his memoirs.

In the fall of 1865, Mac set up winter quarters in the town of Dresden, Germany. In mid-October, Mrs. Marcy and her daughter Fanny visited the McClellans while they were living in Germany. This visit was more than just a social call, for Mrs. McClellan was due to deliver her second child during the month of November, and she wanted her mother to be present for the birth. On November 23, 1865, Ellen gave birth to a healthy baby boy that they affectionately called "Max," although his formal name was George Brinton McClellan, Jr.

The proud father, wrote home to his aging mother with the good news about the birth. Mac told her, "The boy is a dear little fellow—strong and bright—he looks about him as wisely as a young owl and bids fair to be a good specimen."

George McClellan decided to continue touring through Europe during 1866 and 1867, even though he had recently been offered several attractive job offers in the States. For the most part, the McClellans spent their summers in Switzerland and their winters in the south of France. During much of this time, Mac's wife, Ellen, struggled with poor health. The homeopathic doctors that she frequented often recommended that she take advantage of the excellent mineral baths and spas of Europe. Over time, these age old remedies began to help her condition to improve.

During the fall of 1867, George McClellan obtained his first genuine employment since he resigned his military commission in November 1864. Mac went to work for an American marine engineer by the name of Edwin A. Stevens. The contract that McClellan signed in Paris commissioned him to locate a European buyer for a giant iron-clad vessel that Stevens was building. Mac would, naturally, have his expenses covered as he traveled across Europe trying to find a foreign government who was willing to buy this expensive ocean-going war vessel, known as the "Stevens' Battery."

Although the reputation of George McClellan opened up many doors with foreign military leaders and government officials, it did not necessarily make it easy for Mac to negotiate a sale for the Stevens Battery. The leaders in Europe were understandably leery of investing in any venture that had as shaky a history as the vessel designed by Edwin Stevens. Not even George McClellan could satisfactorily explain why the Stevens Battery still lay uncompleted after almost thirty-five years of time and millions of dollars had been spent on it. After months of effort, McClellan had to report to Edwin Stevens that he had not been able to secure a buyer for his craft.

One of the fringe benefits afforded to George McClellan during his meetings with high ranking military officials throughout Europe, was that he could also gain a great deal of insights regarding famous European military campaigns directly from the people who made them happen. This interesting information would often find its way into the articles that Mac was asked to write for newspapers throughout Europe and the United States. As we have already noted, George McClellan was a life-long student of military history and tactics. Consequently, his opinions regarding military events were often in demand right up to the point of his death.

During the spring of 1868, Mac wrote a letter to his old friend, William Prime, confessing, "I am becoming very homesick and tired of this rambling life and Europe." A few months later, McClellan was able to secure a new position with the company run by Edwin Stevens. This time, however, Mac's responsibilities would require him to move back to the United States so he could directly oversee the completion of the Stevens Battery as chief engineer.

On September 29, George McClellan sailed into New York harbor with his family. Three days after Mac arrived, the war veterans from the McClellan Legion staged a grand review down Fifth Avenue. A deeply grateful George McClellan, watched the passing columns from his hotel balcony and instantly knew that his countrymen had not forgotten him. According to the local newspapers the audience that came out to welcome the former commander of the Army of the Potomac "swelled in rising accumulating tides into Madison Square from dusk till nearly midnight."

McClellan also attended a huge Democratic rally in Philadelphia on October 8, where he received a stupendous ovation from the party faithful. This time around, however, Mac would take a much more low-key posture in the business of politics. He already had enough enemies and he desired not to stir up old animosities if at all possible. The major priority in McClellan's life at this time was to reestablish himself as an honorable and successful businessman.

Shortly after reaching the United States, Mac learned that his employer, Edwin Stevens, had recently died, but his will still designated one million dollars to be spent toward the completion of the battery. Mac, therefore, proceeded to take his position as project director as originally planned and moved his family to a home in Hoboken, New Jersey. For the next eighteen months, Mac faithfully worked on the unruly vessel and brought it close to completion. Sadly, however, the money that Stevens had earmarked for the project ran out and work on the vessel once again floundered. Mac was forced to resign from the bankrupt company as no individual or government was willing to invest additional funds towards the vessel's completion. Twelve years later, the "Stevens Battery" project was scrapped, literally!

George McClellan received a number of excellent job offers during the early part of 1870, including a position as the president of the University of California. After careful consideration, however, Mac decided to work as an engineer for the New York City Department of Docks. This position, along with an additional job as the president of the Atlantic and Great Western Railroad, permitted George McClellan to become fairly wealthy for the first time in his life. As a result of the financial blessings that came from Mac's business endeavors, he was able to build a marvelous home on Orange Mountain, New Jersey. The McClellans often called their rambling estate, Maywood, after their first daughter.

After three years of working for the city of New York, George McClellan decided to resign his position with the Department of Docks. He proceeded to establish his own engineering and accounting firm for the primary purpose of representing the interests of European investors who held railroad securities in the United States. McClellan and company promised to help "endangered" stockholders from Europe to properly manage, or if necessary, liquidate their investments.

During the month of October, 1873, Mac once again set sail for Europe in the hopes of introducing his new company to securities holders and banking institutions throughout that continent. This particular trip by George McClellan and family, lasted a period of two years. It was a trip that combined business with pleasure, as the McClellans took time for sightseeing and the usual visits to the premier spas of Europe.

Perhaps the most interesting part of this two-year trip was the five-month excursion that the McClellans took to Egypt. George McClellan was well read in the field of Egyptology and was delighted to have the opportunity to sail up the Nile and to tour through the pyramids and temples of ancient Egypt. Mac recorded in his diary the fact that he met his old war-time colleague, General Charles P. Stone, while touring through Cairo. Stone had left the United States after the war for much the same reason as George McClellan. General Stone was yet another victim of the infamous Secretary of War, Edwin Stanton, and his destructive propaganda. During the brief and pleasant meeting of these two men, Mac discovered that his old acquaintance now worked as the chief of staff to the Khedive[4] of Egypt. He was, from Mac's perspective, a sight for sore eyes.

The only thing about Egypt that was really disappointing to George McClellan was the ground transportation or camels. "These beasts could never hold a candle to my old black charger, Dan Webster," exclaimed the feisty American called "Little Mac."

As the McClellan family continued on their journey, they returned to the business of visiting the major cities of Europe. Mac also continued to write articles for well-known American magazines such as *Harper's Weekly* and the *North American Review*. These articles touched upon a variety of issues related to the science of modern warfare and the military trends in Europe.

During the fall of 1875, the McClellan's returned to their beautiful estate at Orange Mountain, New Jersey. Mac and his family had no sooner become adjusted to life in the States, when the Democratic Party began to re-enlist his support. Unlike the old days, however, Mac would finally feel comfortable in the role of speaking publicly for Democratic candidates. This new confidence was born out of the understanding that his old war time enemies were no longer in power and it was also fueled by the fact that Mac truly respected the Democratic candidate for the 1876 election, Mr. Samuel J. Tilden.

In keeping with his role as party leader, George McClellan gave speeches at over seven cities in the eastern part of the United States during 1876. The theme that McClellan presented to his audience was the aftermath of the War Between the States. He acknowledged

---

4. Title of the Turkish viceroys of Egypt from 1867 to 1914.

his personal gratification for the end of slavery during his talks and stressed the importance of not permitting the issue of black suffrage to stand in the way of sectional harmony and the proper resumption of states' rights. Mac reminded his listeners that Americans in the South had accepted all of the laws imposed upon them and that the time was right for all Americans to have their "rights, privileges, and duties under the Constitution fully restored."

During his talks, Mac would frequently condemn as unjust and unsuccessful the "reconstruction" policies that had been foisted upon the South by radical Republicans. He also made a point of warning his fellow citizens that the spirit of sectionalism would again raise it's ugly head unless the politicians in Washington were willing to abandon their destructive policies. Mac emphasized that "it is only by trusting [the Southerners], treating them kindly, and doing our best to restore kind feeling between all parts of the country, that we can accomplish the real, hearty restoration of the Union which was the true purpose of the war...."

As it turned out, the presidential election between Samuel J. Tilden and Republican Rutherford B. Hayes was very close. Tilden wound up with a slight edge in terms of the popular vote, but Hayes came out ahead in the all-important category of electoral votes. The Electoral Commission ultimately decided in favor of Rutherford Hayes and he soon took the oath as President of the United States.

In spite of a busy political agenda, Mac was able to resume work on his memoirs during 1876. He wrote to a number of his former staff officers and men in an effort to clarify details about past battles and to jog his own memory regarding past events. On a few occasions the former head of the Army of the Potomac met with his old war comrades face to face. These meetings were always a source of particular joy for George McClellan as he was able to relive the amazing experiences that he faced on the field of battle. A clear indication of how much Mac loved to meet with his former soldiers, is seen in the fact that he often permitted these meetings to last until almost midnight. Under normal circumstances, the disciplined and regimented McClellan would rarely forsake his normal bedtime schedule for the sake of a social call.

The engineering and accounting firm that George McClellan established had often experienced it's share of ups and downs. For this reason, Mac typically held an additional job of some kind with one of the railroads or with the public works department of a major city. In addition to these business pursuits, Mac continued to keep his hand in the business of politics as well. George McClellan's political prospects took a decided turn for the better during the fall of 1877. In a move that surprised almost everyone, the Democratic Party in New Jersey unanimously selected Mac to be their gubernatorial candidate during their state convention. When George McClellan received the news of his nomination he immediately accepted the opportunity. Mac confessed to the newspapers that he knew that his name would probably be submitted for consideration during the convention but that, frankly, he felt the possibility of being chosen was remote.

McClellan's prompt acceptance of the nomination from the Democratic Party was in keeping with his lifelong view that he must never turn down an opportunity to do his patriotic duty. Mac believed that such appointments or promotions were, in fact, sent directly from the hand of Almighty God. Candidate McClellan was now 50 years old and welcomed the opportunity to continue doing his civic duty and to be useful in God's service.

The McClellan campaign for governor was soon in full swing. During September and October, Mac had the pleasure of speaking before large crowds of zealous supporters as he toured various cities throughout New Jersey. During one of the campaign rallies, a member of the press asked Mac to explain what he felt was the secret to his popularity. McClellan stated, "I don't remember ever to have done more than my duty.... When I hear the shouts of a crowd like this outside my carriage window, and realize that I am the occasion of it all, I feel as though I were traveling in an unknown world. It's like a dream...." Regardless of the enthusiastic sentiments of candidate McClellan, the truth was that Mac was not dreaming. He was,

in fact, reaping a harvest of honor that had been denied him for far too long. The Lord finally gave George McClellan favor in the people's eyes, and Mac hardly knew how to take it all in.

Not everyone in the state of New Jersey, however, was prepared to treat George McClellan with respect and dignity. The famous political cartoonist Thomas Nast took the opportunity to prepare an uncomplimentary, and yet humorous picture (*above*) of McClellan spying the New Jersey shore while signaling for more Democratic voters to reinforce his ranks.

On election day in November, however, it was candidate McClellan who had the last laugh. He won the election by almost 13,000 votes and soon began his three-year term as the governor of New Jersey. As one would expect, Governor McClellan's time in office was characterized by conservative fiscal policies designed to reduce the state's indebtedness, and by a distinct lack of political corruption. He was particularly pleased to be able to be instrumental in abolishing the policy of direct state taxing of New Jersey citizens and he also was proud to be able to bring needed reforms to the state militia.

George McClellan was usually only required to go to the state capital at Trenton one day per week to take care of his duties as head of the state. Being a state governor at this time in history was not nearly as time consuming a proposition as it is today. The whole scope and philosophy of state government has gradually changed from the time that George McClellan took office. Americans in the 1870s, whether Democrat or Republican, generally believed in the principle of limiting the powers of government to certain constitutional functions. As a

Governor George McClellan

consequence, the demands or expectations of the citizens upon their state leaders was minimal. The people, by and large, believed in the concept of individual responsibility or self-government. They also preferred to turn to the local government as the agency for dealing with local problems, rather than to have to deal with a centralized bureaucracy that was largely unaccountable to the people.

Newspaper reporters throughout New Jersey were frequently impressed by the fact that Governor McClellan was not preoccupied with partisan politics. Mac was careful to promote conservative principles of government as the answer for all Americans, regardless of party affiliation. Governor McClellan's 1879 state of the state address was characterized by the news media "as devoid of party allusion and party spirit as one of Paul's epistles."

As Mac's term of office was about to expire in early 1881, he wrote his mother stating that he was glad that his duties as governor would soon be over as it was "becoming a nuisance to be obligated to go to Trenton in all matters." True to form, George McClellan had no interest in using his public office as a means to establish a political Tower of Babel. He was happy to serve and he was also happy to step aside and give others the opportunity to serve. In this respect, Governor McClellan showed himself to be more than a mere politician; he was a statesman.

At this point in McClellan's life, he possessed a genuine sense of accomplishment as he looked back upon the last three years of public service. He also possessed a very real desire to take his family on holiday to St. Moritz, France. This time, however, Mac would be able to leave his beloved homeland with his head held high and with no regrets. The McClellans set sail for Europe during April of 1881. This family vacation would keep George McClellan in Europe until the fall of the year.

If Mac had any concerns about how he might keep busy upon his return to the states, those considerations were resolved in dramatic and tragic fashion. George McClellan soon learned, after arriving in New York, that the warehouse that he had placed his prized collection of china and ceramics in prior to going oversees had burned down. To make matters worse, Mac had also stored his only copy of his completed memoirs in this same storage facility and it was totally destroyed. "I have not the heart to begin," wrote McClellan to a close friend who was trying to urge him to reconstruct his writings.

Within several months, however, Mac summoned the courage to resume work on his memoirs. Over the next few years, George McClellan labored in an unsystematic and more limited manner on his manuscript. Most of Mac's reconstructed writings would center upon his military experiences during the War Between the States. As a result, numerous details of his life before and after the civil war would never be revealed to the public. These details were only included within his original manuscript that was burnt to ashes.

By this time in McClellan's life, he knew how necessary it was to persevere through tragedy and hardships. The former general and governor, therefore, went about the business of living and raising a family in spite of disappointments. He lived with his wife and children in New York during the wintertime and spent the rest of the year at his estate on Orange Mountain. Mrs. Ellen McClellan still loved to entertain guests while in New York and hardly a week went by without some special social event being held in their home near Gramercy Park.

George McClellan's business ventures continued to be numerous and varied from 1881 to 1885. He was on the board of several prestigious companies and held a considerable number of stocks and bonds. The success that McClellan realized in the business field, however, often left him bored and restless. Mac's daughter, May, wrote in her diary for May 7, 1882, the following, "Papa and I went to Doctor Crosby's church today. I am worried about him; he is so depressed—if he only had something to do that would occupy his mind."

During the presidential race of 1884, Mac once again found that the arena of politics afforded him the intellectual stimulation that his active mind craved. He worked diligently during the fall of 1884 to help the Democratic presidential candidate Grover Cleveland to become the next occupant of the White House. For a change, Mac's efforts along with the labors of the Democrats at large, met with success. Grover Cleveland was the first conservative Democrat to be elected President since before the War Between the States. Mac was hopeful that this political victory would usher in a new era for the nation. He also prayed that it would open up the opportunity for him to receive an appointment to President Cleveland's cabinet as the Secretary of War.

Sources close to the new President went so far as to give Mac "positive assurance" that the Cabinet position would be offered to him. Needless to say, however, almost nothing is a sure thing when it comes to political appointments. A controversy soon developed between Democratic forces from within the state of New Jersey regarding who should be given the post of Secretary of War. This controversy finally culminated in the decision by President Cleveland to select someone for the coveted cabinet post from outside of New Jersey. Although George McClellan was disappointed by the manner in which President Cleveland reached his decision, he still managed to handle this situation gracefully. It was against Mac's principles to directly solicit a position within the government. As a consequence, the elder statesman for the Democratic party would not wind up working with the Cleveland Administration.

Chapter Thirteen

The Roll Is Called Up Yonder

1885

Early in 1885, George McClellan had two articles published in *The Century* magazine as a part of their "Battles and Leaders of the Civil War" series. Mac was asked to write about his experiences as a commander during the Peninsula and Maryland campaigns. These articles contained a number of interesting accounts of private conversations that McClellan had with President Lincoln and Secretary of War Stanton. They also revealed some of the reasons why the North was unable to defeat the South during 1861 and 1862.

George McClellan was also pleased to receive an invitation to speak at a Decoration Day reunion that was to be held on May 30 at the Antietam battlefield cemetery. Mac's participation in this special gathering would mark the first and last time that the former head of the Army of the Potomac would return to the battleground at Antietam.

During the morning of May 30, 1885, George McClellan toured the battlefield grounds with a former member of Stonewall Jackson's staff by the name of Henry Kyd Douglas. As both men walked together, they engaged in good-humored criticism of each other and no doubt talked about the multitude of mutual friends that had fallen at Antietam almost 23 years before. For the first time in recent memory, a large delegation of veterans from the South had crossed over the river with Douglas primarily to meet with and listen to the not-so-young Napoleon.

Later in the afternoon, George McClellan made his way to the speakers' platform and prepared to address an audience made up primarily of veterans from the North and South. McClellan opened his talk by reminding the soldiers that, "The smoke of battle still wreaths these hills and fills these valleys, these rocks still re-echo the harsh sounds of strife, and the ground was all too thickly strewn with the forms of the quiet dead, and of those still writhing in agony."

As Mac continued to address the men who were now assembled together in peace, he spoke to them all as his countrymen. "Let us bury all animosity, all bitter recollections of the past.... We now have a common purpose to testify our reverence for the valiant dead," stated McClellan. He went on to acknowledge the "noble Robert E. Lee, and the men who were clad in grey." Mac also spoke affectionately of the Army of the Potomac, "so very dear to me..., ever worthy of its fame, whether in adversity or success—and never more so than on this field...."

Toward the close of his speech, George McClellan confessed, "I am glad, inexpressibly glad, that I have been permitted to live until the fame and exploits of these magnanimous rivals have become the common property of our people; when the ability and virtues of Robert E. Lee, and the achievement of the magnificent Army of Northern Virginia, as well as the heroism and renown of the proud Army of the Potomac, have already become a part of the common heritage of glory of the people of America."

As the final words gracefully fell from the lips of the old soldier from New Jersey, the veterans of the blue and grey rose and marched together before the reviewing stand. Mac intently watched the long columns pass before him, while he returned a continual stream of salutes. The men who had fought for General McClellan must have been very proud of their former leader as they marched past and remembered how he had made them into an army capable of victory. The soldiers in grey undoubtedly had a great deal of passionate thoughts at this time as well as they remembered the exploits of men like Stonewall Jackson and A. P. Hill.

Newspapers across the country heralded McClellan's speech as a work of art that would echo down the corridors of time. One newspaper reporter who heard Mac's address wrote that "General

McClellan's oration was a scholarly production, and was delivered with an ease and grace of manner and speech that were cordially recognized. He was awarded several rousing cheers at the close."

In late August 1885, George McClellan boarded a train with his aged father-in-law, Randolph Marcy, headed for the Red River country of Texas. This area was originally explored by these two seasoned gentlemen in 1852. They were returning to this part of the country to inspect a mining venture that Mac was interested in pursuing. Both men thoroughly enjoyed the trek west, which included stops in distant locations such as Denver, Salt Lake City, and San Francisco. At almost every place they stopped, old veterans would come out to the station and enthusiastically greet them.

Randolph Marcy and George McClellan returned to their homes on September 17, in order to celebrate the twenty-third anniversary of the battle of Antietam. During this time frame, Mac renewed his efforts to complete his memoirs as he relaxed in his Orange Mountain estate. The trip that McClellan took to the Western states left him uncharacteristically tired and he welcomed the opportunity to rest and recharge his energy.

In early October, however, Mac began to experience severe chest pains that were diagnosed as angina pectoris. McClellan's doctor prescribed various treatments and rest. Within a week or two Mac appeared to be doing considerably better and his doctor felt that he would make a complete recovery. Nevertheless, on the evening of October 28, while finishing an article for *The Century*, McClellan began to experience severe chest pains once again. His condition quickly deteriorated through the hours of the night, and at three o'clock the next morning, he turned and looked in the direction of his beloved wife and whispered to his physician, "Tell her I am better now. Thank you." A few moment later, George McClellan went home to be with the Lord. He was only 58 years old.

The story of George McClellan's passing was plastered on the front page of newspapers across the United States and in Europe. President Grover Cleveland and numerous dignitaries sent messages of condolence to Ellen McClellan. Military leaders from the North and South also expressed deep regret at the unexpected passing of this noble gentleman. August Belmont was quoted as saying that the country had lost "one of her purest and most patriotic sons." The famous Confederate general, P. G. T. Beauregard, made it clear that he respected Mac "as a man and soldier." General Joe Johnston, who fought with McClellan in Mexico, and against him during the War Between the States, told the reporters that he would surely miss "a dear friend whom I have so long loved and admired."

Detailed obituaries summarized and eulogized the incredible accomplishments of the former commander of the Army of the Potomac. Although some newspapers could not resist criticizing George McClellan for his failures, nearly every public sentiment was quick to acknowledge Mac's phenomenal organizational talents and exemplary character. The *New York World* was one of the few newspapers to set forth a truly accurate analysis of the legacy of George McClellan, "No General who fought in the war from its outbreak to its close was ever actuated by nobler sentiments and purer and more patriotic motives. Yet no soldier was ever more unjustly dealt with or more harshly, cruelly, and unfairly criticized."

A simple and brief funeral service took place on November 2 at the Madison Square Presbyterian Church in New York, where George McClellan had been a member until he became a ruling elder at the Presbyterian church in Orange, New Jersey. Clouds and rain greeted the mourners as they poured out of the church building en route to the McClellan and Marcy family plot at the Riverview Cemetery in Trenton. The list of honorary pallbearers read like a "Who's Who" from the military and business realms. General McClellan's trusted army friends such as Fitz John Porter, William Franklin, and Winfield Scott Hancock were among those selected to carry Mac's remains along with the beloved Joe Johnston. Faithful friends from civilian life like Samuel Barlow, William Prime, and Abram Hewitt were also present to pay their last respects to their fallen comrade.

The gathering at the cemetery was under the direction of the pastor from the Madison Square Presbyterian Church. He offered up a prayer at the graveside which reminded the audience that all Christians have the sure hope and promise of eventual resurrection and eternal life. This servant of God also encouraged those who were in the faith by assuring them that they would one day see their departed friend in the joyful place called heaven. As the large crowd began to depart from the graveside of George Brinton McClellan, they looked out over the rambling Delaware River. No one in the assembly seemed to notice or care that McClellan had just as many friends at his funeral from the South as he did from the North. This is undoubtedly the way that the departed soldier and patriot would have wanted it.

Statuette of General George B. McClellan by J. A. Bailly

Epilogue

O ne of the more interesting obituaries for George Brinton McClellan contained a suggestion for an epitaph for his gravestone. "History will do him justice," was the optimistic phrase that appeared in the *World* newspaper obituary column shortly after McClellan's death.

This provocative epitaph begs the question, "has history done General McClellan justice?" The answer should, by this point, be rather obvious. No.

For well over a century, the reputation of George McClellan has been torn to shreds by historians and authors who have passionately disagreed with Mac's view of the abolitionist movement and his biblical approach to war. This is not to say that General McClellan's life is above criticism. Anyone studying the life of this influential American can see that he did not always take the right stand. His sins, however, were covered by the blood of Christ his Savior and he lived in the light that God gave to his generation. Mac served God, family, and country faithfully throughout his adult life and his legacy, therefore, deserves to be honored.

True American patriots and godly role models are always in short supply. It is very important, therefore, for modern historians and students of history to refuse to join ranks with those that denigrate the memory of great men, such as George McClellan, simply because they failed to measure up to modern notions of political correctness.

George McClellan's widow Ellen moved abroad to Europe shortly after her husband's death. She spent a great deal of the remainder of her life in Europe. Mrs. McClellan died in 1915 at the age of seventy-nine while visiting her daughter, May, in the town of Nice, France. George McClellan's son, Max, became a distinguished American statesman in his own right. He served as a congressman from New York from 1895 to 1903 and as the mayor of New York

City from 1903 to 1909. Max McClellan was married in 1889, but the Lord did not choose to bless his family with children. George McClellan's son died in 1940 and his daughter died childless in 1945.

Bibliography

Angle, Paul M. *Tragic Years 1860–1865*. New York: Simon and Schuster, 1960.

Bailey, Ronald H. *Forward to Richmond: McClellan's Peninsular Campaign*. Virginia: Time-Life Books, 1983.

Castle, John. *Battles and Leaders of the Civil War Volumes 1–4*. New Jersey: Book Sales, Inc., 1976.

Curtis, George Ticknor. *McClellan's Last Service to the Republic, Together with a Tribute to His Memory*. New York: D. Appleton and Company, 1886.

Dabney, R. L. *Life and Campaigns of Lieut.-General Thomas J. Jackson*. 1865. Harrisonburg, Virginia: Sprinkle Publications, 1983 reprint.

Henty, G. A. *With Lee In Virginia*. Pennsylvania: Preston-Speed Publishers, 1997 reprint.

McClellan, George Brinton. *McClellan's Own Story*. Edited by William C. Prime. New York: Charles L. Webster and Company, 1887.

McClellan, George Brinton. *The Civil War Papers of George B. McClellan: Selected Correspondence, 1860–1865*. Edited by Stephen W. Sears. New York: Ticknor and Fields, 1989.

McClellan, George Brinton. *The Mexican War Diary of George B. McClellan*. Edited by William Starr Myers. Princeton, NJ: Princeton University Press, 1917.

Myers, William Starr. *General George Brinton McClellan: A Study In Personality*. New York: D. Appleton-Century Company, 1934.

Robertson, James I., Jr. *General A. P. Hill: The Story of a Confederate Warrior*. New York: Random House, 1987

Sears, Stephen W., *George B. McClellan: The Young Napoleon.* New York: Ticknor & Fields, 1988.

Warner, Ezra. *Generals in Blue: Lives of the Union Commanders.* Louisiana State University Press, 1964.

Waugh, John C. *The Class of 1846.* New York: Warner Books, Inc., 1994.

Wheeler, Richard. *Sword Over Richmond.* New York: Harper and Row Publisher, 1986.

Wilkins, Steven. *Call of Duty: The Sterling Nobility of Robert E. Lee.* Elkton, Maryland: Holly Hall Publications, 1997.

Williamson, Mary L. *The Life of General Thomas J. Jackson.* 1895. Edited by Michael J. McHugh. Arlington Heights, Illinois: Christian Liberty Press, 1997 reprint.

Williamson, Mary L. *The Life of J. E. B. Stuart.* 1903. Edited by Michael J. McHugh. Arlington Heights, Illinois: Christian Liberty Press, 1996 reprint.

Picture Credits

Digital Stock, American Civil War collection—11, 47, 78, 91, 95, 99, 102, 140, 163

Eleanor S. Brockenbrough Library, The Museum of the Confederacy, Richmond, Virginia—38

James L. Marks Gallery, Kennesaw, Georgia—159

John Hay Library, Brown University—196

Library of Congress—2, 39, 69, 72, 80, 88, 92

National Archives—27, 151

Special Collections Division, U.S. Military Academy Library—6

Vermont Historical Society—101

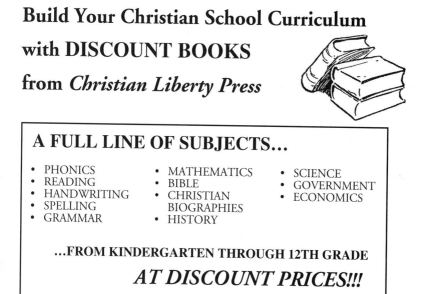